This Change Is Everything

The Hope and Future of Gospel Mission

SHANE SEBASTIAN

This Change Is Everything
Published by Cru Press

100 Lake Hart Drive 2500
Orlando, FL 32832

Cru Press is the publishing division of the Campus Ministry of Cru.

Design by Aaron Martin
www.iamaaronmartin.com
Cover photo by Joshua Earle
Back cover photo by Jake Melara

Editor: Austin Ross
Copyediting: Christina Marty

Additional copies:
www.crupress.com
1-800-827-2788

ISBN number: 1-57334-103-7

WHAT OTHERS ARE SAYING

"Shane Sebastian has written a book about The Missing Beatitude from the eight Jesus gave in the Sermon on the Mount. The missing Ninth Beatitude is 'Blessed are the World Changers.' The Story of the Bible is of young people being "sent" by God to do great things beyond their abilities or even aspiration. To activate your 'sentness' as a world-changer, this is the book for you."

Leonard Sweet

Best-selling author, professor (George Fox University, Drew University, Tabor College), and founder of preachthestory.com

"Written in the rich spiritual heritage of John Mott, Henrietta Mears, and Dr. Bill Bright, Shane Sebastian penned a must read for every college student serious about the gospel of Jesus Christ, and the mandate of the Great Commission."

Rick Soto

Pastor, The Ranch Church

"Visionary and Biblical. Motivating stories of young men and women who have proactively advanced the greatest movement in history. And practical—Shane tackles the most difficult hindrances, with chapters on discerning God's will and relating to family who may not understand our passion for Christ. A must read book for every college student before they graduate. I love it!"

Roger Hershey

Cru National Speaker, Author of *The Finishers*

"Shane beautifully intertwines what God is doing through young adults now in missions and what God has done through young adults in previous generations to make a strong case that God most strategic resource in furthering missions is young people. If you wrestle with God's call or have ever considered serving in missions short-term or long term, this book is for you!"

Holly Melton

Speaker and author of *Follow My Lead: Responding to God's voice in Everyday Encounters*

"I'll never forget the night I responded to an altar call and prayed, 'Here am I, send me.' It was a prayer that God honored and used to launch a lifelong adventure of serving Christ. In *This Change is Everything*, Shane makes a compelling case for God's heart for missions and effectively summons you to pray that same prayer. Warning, reading this book could turn into the adventure of a lifetime."

Dr. Douglas Witherup

Executive Director of Church Ministries,
NC Assemblies of God

"As a youth pastor I loved challenging students with the words that Paul wrote to Timothy that said 'Don't let anyone look down on your youthfulness.' This book not only unpacks what that means, but specifically and strategically shows students how to step by step apply it to their lives."

Chris Brown

Senior Pastor at North Coast Church

"Mobilizing younger generations of Christians to make disciples of all people groups in the world is crucial for the advancement of the Kingdom of God. Shane clearly lays out the Biblical foundation for this mobilization, its challenges, and common-sense solutions that will help countless Christians fulfill the Great Commission."

Kelly Nichols

Director of Student Missions, Colorado Christian University

"Dr. Shane Sebastian has devoted years investing in leading university students in international contexts; Shane has passion for Jesus, family, friends, and students as well as a well-honed character. For students and leaders desiring to cross cultures to share Jesus, Dr. Sebastian is a sure guide and faithful fellow pilgrim."

Dr. Loren Kerns, Ph.D.

"For any student looking to live for the mission of God- this is the book you have been waiting for! A brilliant survey of the past and a compelling 'how-to' for future world changers."

Dr. Todd Ahrend

Founder, The Traveling Team

"Research shows that most people who follow Jesus make that decision when they the young. The importance of reaching children at an early age cannot be overstated. Shane Sebastian's book *This Change is Everything* shares how God has used young people throughout history to advance the Kingdom and helps us to not only understand the importance of reaching young people for Christ, but also to challenge our youth to reach out to their peers around the world and make a difference!"

Josh D. McDowell

Author, Speaker

TO MOM AND DAD

Thank you for showing me how to hear and obey the voice of the Lord.

Then I heard the voice of the Lord saying, "Whom shall I send? And who will go for us?"

And I said, "Here am I. Send me!"
Isaiah 6:8

ACKNOWLEDGEMENTS

Though this book started in my doctoral studies, it has come out of several decades of working with young people around the world.

Thank you first to my wife, Laura. Twenty-one years of marriage has been such a gift to me. You are a blessing to our four awesome children. Kirra, you are a light to everyone around you. Summer, you are so thoughtful. David, I love your passion for the ocean. Curren, you are the best traveler I know, and I love going places with you!

Thanks so much to my doctoral cohort in seminary. You have provided not just encouragement in my studies and walk with Jesus, but lasting friendship. I have had so much fun growing as friends.

To the team at George Fox: Len, you have helped me help others "read the signs." Cliff and Loren, thank you for your leadership and guidance. Laura, thank you for helping me in my writing and research.

When I was a junior in college, God led me to a couple, Jamey and Gretchen Pappas. You two are some of the best leaders I know. Knowing you and growing in our friendship is a life-long gift to me.

Thank you to my team of supporters who help Laura and me do what we do in helping young people understand Jesus Christ.

TABLE OF CONTENTS

FORWARD

Every day I see articles about how your generation is in trouble. How you can't survive at work or you're too attached to your parents or too selfish, too connected, or not connected enough.

I don't believe those things, because I've worked with people like you for years. I've seen young people do incredible, unexpected, amazing things. I know that you look at the world and see how it is broken, how there are things that need to be changed, and you're sizing it up, figuring out the best way to start fixing things.

In the midst of all these pronouncements of doom about your generation, I think you'll find Shane Sebastian's book *This Change is Everything* to be something different and refreshing. Shane doesn't just believe that young people can change the world, he thinks you're by far the best people to do it. He believes in you. He believes that your insights, your hard work and your desire to make the world a better place are actually going to change things.

It's entirely possible that you don't believe that yourself. You may look at the world you're inheriting and find it laughable that anyone would try to wade in and make things better. You might think you're not good enough, or smart enough, or talented enough or insightful enough to make things better.

Shane is going to prove you wrong in this book.

I've known Shane for a lot of years, and he's one of the most authentic, kind and honest people I know. He loves his family, he loves Jesus and he loves surfing. He doesn't blow smoke, he doesn't exaggerate or lie about his feelings. When he writes a sentence, it's something he believes with his whole heart. There's not a single word in this book that he doesn't earnestly believe it true, and in the end this book is about one core belief of Shane's: he believes you can, through God's power, be the person who changes the world for the better.

In this book, Shane is going to walk us through the history of God using young people to transform individuals, communities, cultures and nations. He's going to show us how those enormous obstacles we see that we think prevent us from being a part of changing the world -- things like parents being worried about you leaving the country, money, debt, getting a job -- are not obstacles so much as opportunities to see God at work. He's going to walk us through the Bible and show us that God, too, looks on young people as special servants who he is particularly pleased to work alongside.

That's an important thing about this book. God is going to speak to your through it. I'd encourage you to listen carefully, to read prayerfully, and to ask yourself after each chapter, "What is God saying to me?" If you do those things, I trust that the words Shane shares here will be transformative, life-giving and inspiring.

So, the book you're holding... it might just change your life. Don't read on unless you're willing to be challenged, to be changed, and to come to a crossroads where you seriously have to ask yourself how God wants you to be involved in transforming the world.

I hope you'll read this book. It's going to change your life. And Shane and I and so many others believe you are going to change the world. We need you. We're looking forward to seeing what God will do through you.

Matt Mikalatos

INTRODUCTION

"*Tengo una reunion con muchos estudiantes hoy.*" I struggled through a few sentences as I tried to convince a security guard to let me on campus at the University of Puerto Rico. As I stuttered through my Spanish I showed him a stack of cards representing students who indicated they would like to speak with someone about what it means to know God and to participate in a small group Bible study. After a few minutes of trying to explain who I was, what I was doing, and even flashing my business card (like that was going to do anything) he actually let me park and go on campus.

I walked to the university center and began to text dozens of students who had filled out spiritual interest surveys. By the end of that day I met with five students. Two had prayed with me to become Christians. The next day was similar to the first. All of this spiritual interest was pointing to these students searching for something, anything, that would give them meaning and purpose in life.

In seminary, I studied semiotics. I never heard of it until I studied it. Semiotics is simply reading signs. Jesus spoke of the importance of being able to read the signs of our culture. He said, "You know how to interpret the appearance of the sky, but you cannot interpret the signs of the times" (Matthew 16:2-3). Author and friend, Leonard Sweet, likes to say, "We are directed by Jesus to learn how to read signs, to read the handwriting on the wall." Semiotics is to help others see what God is doing around them.

Think about the signs of our times. What are the most popular television programs? Reality TV! This fascination with reality TV is an obvious sign that people are looking for authenticity and transparency. They are looking for *something real*. Seeing this is called *semiotic awareness*.

Semiotics is like missions. A missionary simply helps someone from another culture understand how God is working around them; they point out God's writing in their lives. Over the past several thousand years, young people have been great semioticians. They have helped others – in different cultures all around the world – understand what God is doing around them. Young people in the Bible, from start to finish, pointed others to salvation in Christ. This legacy continued in the early centuries and into the last several hundred years of global missions advancement. It really is amazing how God has used young people to advance his kingdom. Young people, as you will read throughout this book, have always made great missionaries.

Today's young people are no different.

This book is written with you in mind. God wants us all to be missionaries. He wants us to help others, even in cultures different from our own, to see and understand how he is working. You have been called to be a semiotician, to be a missionary. I hope this book helps you on this journey.

The first half of this book will be spent diving into the history of young people's amazing impact on world missions. The second half of the book dives into the main obstacles they face as they consider crossing cultures and sharing the reality of Jesus Christ with people around the world. Through it all you will see how God has indeed made you a world changer.

CHAPTER 1

YOUR PART IN HIS STORY

"The Bible recounts how God has used people of all ages and backgrounds to advance His purposes. Many of the most remarkable events of the biblical story involved young people. It should not be surprising to find that in recent centuries, many of the greatest things God has done to fulfill the Great Commission have been done with university students."
David Howard, *Student Power in World Missions*

"Drink! Drink! Drink!"

"Come on Shane, just a few shots with us. Let's loosen up a bit."

Welcome to college.

A few hours earlier, my parents dropped me off for my first year of higher education. After saying goodbye, I went with my roommates to the cafeteria. I couldn't believe all the food available and that I didn't have to clean the dishes. It was awesome. My new friends and I ate a ridiculous amount of food—very healthy calories like brownies and french fries—and then went and participated in what would take a considerable amount of our time that first year of college: playing video games.

After investing too much time trying to impress my roommates with my gaming skills, we headed back up to our new home for the year, a 12-by-12 foot dorm room with two small windows. As we turned the corner and walked closer, we heard noise. Loud, thumping, bass-filled noise. I walked in my room and entered a scene that would not be uncommon that first year: lights flashing (where did those come from?), friends sitting on my bed (I sleep there, people, get off my bed), dirty clothes on the floor (how did those get there? I had barely moved in) and a traffic jam getting in and out of the door.

And one more significant thing: lots of liquor.

My neighbor, John, who organized the party and eventually became a good friend that year, offered me a shot of vodka and orange juice.

I was terrified. I didn't want to accept the drink. But I didn't want to look stupid, either. I remember feeling a hand tap on my shoulder, "Hey Shane, my name is Ethan. Do you have a minute?"

That minute changed my life.

THE STORY

Ethan eventually asked if I would like to attend a Bible study with him during orientation week. I'm not kidding.

I'm pretty sure God orchestrated that.

I was actually really nervous when I walked into that first Bible study. As I looked around the room, my anxiety level dropped when I saw that the study had quite a few more girls than guys. I guess I thought it was a good place to make some new "friends," because I decided to stay.

Even more than the girls in that Bible study, I remember what I learned. I learned of the continuity of the story of the Bible. The Bible was written over a fifteen-hundred-year span. It was written on three different continents, and in three different languages. Yet with all of this diversity, there is one main story in the Bible: God's love for every person in every culture.

I learned that God's desire to know and be known by his creation is clearly written throughout the entire Bible. In Scripture, from start to finish, we see that God's mission - *his Story* - is to be known among all the nations and to have a relationship with his creation.

The Story Introduced

In Genesis 10, we read about what is called "the table of nations." The table of nations is exactly what it sounds like: a list of the nations existing during that time. There are seventy nations listed, which was the total of all nations in the world.

Then in Genesis 11 we read a crazy story about how God

actually created the nations that are listed in the previous chapter. At this point in history, there is still only one nation, one culture that God has created: "Now the whole world had one language and a common speech" (Genesis 11:1). We read that these people, this one nation, wanted to build a tower that would show how powerful they were, a tower that would display their greatness. Some Bible scholars say they built this tower because they thought God would destroy them through another flood (as he did in Genesis chapter 4) because they were so wicked.

God did promise that he would never flood the earth again. Yet he was very unhappy with these people. So what did God do? He took this one nation and created seventy nations. Genesis 11:7 says, "'Come, let us go down and confuse their language so they will not understand each other.' So the Lord scattered them from there over all the earth." God literally takes one culture and creates many cultures.

As we move to Genesis 12, we read of an incredible promise—a promise where God involves you and me. God tells Abraham that he is going to be a blessing to the nations, to the whole world. Genesis 12:1-3 says, "The Lord had said to Abram, 'Go from your country, your people and your father's household to the land I will show you. I will make you a great nation, and I will bless you; I will make your name great, and you will be a blessing. I will bless those who bless you, and whoever curses you I will curse, and all the peoples of earth will be blessed through you.'" Again, God promises that he will use Abram (later God changes his name to Abraham) and his family to bless all the nations, all the peoples and cultures God has created.

People Groups, Not Political Borders

In college, I studied Political Science (well, I at least went to lectures about it). I remember one of my professors lecturing on how the nations of the world were in constant change throughout history. New borders would be created and new countries would emerge. He would show maps of the world over time to demonstrate how countries have changed.

But when the Bible speaks of nations, it's not referring to pictures on a map. "Nations" in scripture refers not to political lines, but to unique ethnic groups and languages. When God speaks of his desire to know the nations, he is speaking of knowing the unique cultures he has created.

God introduces his love for the nations in Genesis. But his love for the nations, and his desire to know and be known by all cultures, is repeated throughout the entire Bible. From start to finish, this story is everywhere in the Bible. The main story of the Bible, its theme, is about spreading knowledge of God to all people in every nation and in every language. Bob Sjogren, in his book *Unveiled at Last*, calls this storyline "a unifying thematic backbone permeating God's Word from Genesis to Revelation."

The Story in the Old Testament

The Old Testament speaks of God's heart for the nations. The prophet Habakkuk says, "For the earth will be filled with the knowledge of the glory of the Lord as the waters cover the sea" (Habakkuk 2:14). Isaiah speaks of the glory of God: "You are my servant, Israel, in whom I will show my glory" (Isaiah 40:5). King David writes in 1 Chronicles 16 verses 8 and 23, "Oh give thanks to the Lord, call upon his name; make known his deeds among the peoples ...Sing to the Lord, all the earth, proclaim his salvation day after day. Declare his glory among the *nations*, his marvelous deeds among all peoples." Finally, the prophet Malachi speaks of God's glory: "'For from the rising of the sun even in its setting, My name will be great among the nations, and in every place incense is going to be offered in my name, and a grain offering that is pure; for my name will be great among the *nations*,' says the Lord of hosts" (Malachi 1:11). God's love for every nation is all over the Old Testament.

THE STORY IN THE NEW TESTAMENT

The theme of God desiring to be known by every nation, every people, continues in the New Testament with Jesus giving this charge: "All authority has been given to me in heaven and on earth. Go therefore and make disciples of all the *nations*, baptizing them in the name of the Father and the Son and the Holy

Spirit, teaching them to observe all that I have commanded you; and lo, I am with you always, even to the very end of the age" (Matthew 28:18-20).

This challenge, known as the Great Commission, is given, in varied forms, in the first five books of the New Testament. In Acts 1:8 Jesus speaks of this before he ascends to heaven: "But you will receive power when the Holy Spirit has come upon you; and you shall be my witnesses both in Jerusalem, and in all Judea and Samaria, and even to the remotest part of the earth."

The Conclusion to the Story

I have four kids and they have always enjoyed my wife Laura reading to them aloud. Whether it was *Clifford the Big Red Dog* when they were two, or *The Lord of the Rings* trilogy today, they have always enjoyed a good story. Every good book you read has a strong introduction, a main theme or story, and a dramatic conclusion. The Bible is no different. The introduction to the Bible is the first eleven chapters of Genesis. The story or main theme is clarified in Genesis 12, and the dramatic conclusion is the book of Revelation.

In Revelation 7:9, God concludes the story of the Bible by saying, "After this I looked, and there before me was a great multitude that no one could count, from every nation, tribe, people and language, standing before the throne and before the Lamb."

In the last book of the Bible, after reading of God's heart for the nations throughout the Bible, we see God finish the story with all nations represented in heaven. All of these people had come to know God and his love for them. The question is: how did they all hear about him?

THE STORYTELLERS

Each week, my friend Ethan and I would go back to that Bible study where I learned about the story and the mission of the Bible. Learning of God's love for every culture was new to me. But what was so cool to see was whom God had chosen to advance the plot of the Bible: *young people.*

Again, the story of the Bible is very clear: God's love for all nations and his love for the unique cultures he created. The Bible, and all of history, is also very clear when it comes to those who told the story. From the early days of the Bible through the present, we see example after example of God using young people to bless the nations.

Here are some fascinating facts about the world changers we will look at in this book:

- Some of the greatest leaders and missionaries in the Bible were young people.
- Centuries ago, a shepherd boy named David, who happened to be about seventeen years old, destroyed the greatest warrior in the world. Why, exactly, did he do it? He did it, according to the Bible, to share with the world how great God is. This young man says he did it "to show the *whole world* that there is an extraordinary God in Israel" (1 Samuel 17:46).
- God used a young woman named Esther in the Bible to save an entire culture.
- All but one of the disciples of Jesus Christ, those who eventually spread Christianity, were all young, likely teenagers, when he chose them.
- God called a young man named Patrick at the age of twenty-two to share the story of Jesus in Ireland in the fifth century. The results are almost unbelievable as God used him to reach an entire generation.
- The first missionaries sent from North America were all under twenty-three years old.
- God called a young man, a sophomore from Occidental College in Los Angeles, to share God's story with Indians in southern Mexico. Within a decade he translated the Bible into their language, planted several churches, taught them how to read, and trained them in life-saving health measures.
- The greatest athlete in Great Britain's history gave up his sport to become a missionary. He took his friends to China and shared with people who had never heard of Jesus Christ. He was twenty-two years old.

- A nineteen-year-old from the University of Minnesota dropped out of college, bought a one-way ticket to Colombia, and landed in the jungle without knowing anyone. Just a few years later, an entire tribe had heard of God's love for them, and several became missionaries themselves.

The Stumbling Blocks

When I was a junior in college, I transferred to UC Irvine in Southern California. Living outside of the dorms, I was responsible for shopping and cooking for myself. That year I ate the staple diet for college students worldwide: Top Ramen and macaroni and cheese. Sometimes I even got a little bit crazy and added bacon to my diet.

I lived next door to a married couple named Jamey and Gretchen, who became two of my best friends. It was obvious Gretchen felt sorry for me; she introduced me to salad, fruit, and other healthy foods.

One night over dinner, Jamey asked if I would consider going on a mission trip the following summer. I remember Jamey and Gretchen spoke of how a mission trip could help me both grow in my relationship with God and be a blessing to the nations.

I immediately thought of reasons why I could never do something like that. I thought of the cost of the trip itself. How would I pay for it? I thought of my lack of training. I had never even taken a class on the Bible. Also, what would my parents think? I thought of my need to work during the summer to save money for school. I also thought of God's will. How could I know if this was something God wanted me to do?

The story of the Bible is remarkable. There is a reason why it is referred to as *the good news*. The fact that God created us, and desires to know us, is good news! The good news is that Jesus died for our sins and was raised back to life so that we might live with him forever. I love to help people understand that God has called young people throughout history to tell this story, to tell the good news. Young people. Over the past twenty-five years, I have seen consistent stumbling blocks young people encounter as they consider telling God's story—many are the very same obstacles I faced when I was that age, when I was considering how I could help share God's story. The second half of this book will look in more detail at the four main stumbling blocks young people face as they consider telling God's story to the nations.

Hip Hop for Jesus in Tokyo

Ten years ago, a girl I know, Michelle, went to Japan for a year to work with college students as a missionary. After training, and with an open heart, she began to make friends with students on a campus in Tokyo. She noticed that Japanese students really love their music; they love hip-hop and dancing. So Michelle did something I would never have done in a million years: she started a hip-hop dance club.

A few times a week Michelle, would gather her new friends and they would dance. Michelle would teach, they would practice together, and then go out to eat. After a month or so, a student in the club, Yukina, asked Michelle why exactly she was in Tokyo that year. She said, "I am here to help students like you understand God's love for them. He has changed my life, and he can change yours too."

Fast-forward ten months. Yukina had become a follower of Jesus through her friendship with Michelle. Yukina eventually led her sister and her parents into a relationship with God. The next summer they were baptized as a family. Lives were changed as they heard and understood the story that is so consistent through the Bible—God's heart for the nations.

God wants you to be a major player in his story. He wants to use you to be a blessing to the nations, and to those around you, as Michelle was to Yukina and her family in Japan. This book is written with you in mind. God wants you to understand his story and his love for the nations and cultures he has created. Many of those nations live right here in your own dorm, neighborhood, or school. But be warned, as you come to understand God's heart for the world, your heart will grow as well. You will become a world-changer.

QUESTIONS FOR INDIVIDUAL OR GROUP REFLECTION:

What is the best book you have ever read? What did you enjoy most about the story?

Have you ever thought about the Bible as a complete story? How would you tell it?

Are you surprised at anything you read in this chapter? What is new to you?

What is the most important takeaway from this chapter for you?

CHAPTER 2

CHASING SHEEP AND ARGUING WITH GOD

> "Don't let anyone look down on you because you are young."
> The Apostle Paul to his young protégé Timothy
> 1 Timothy 4:12

Young people make great missionaries. In fact, history has been shaped by young people taking the message of Jesus Christ around the world. As I've heard author Steve Shadrach say, "Every spiritual awakening has been spread by university students."

An example would be my friend, Mike. Mike is a world changer. We met when he was a freshman at UC Santa Barbara. He is currently an accounts manager of a software company and living outside of San Francisco. During his freshman year, Mike grew deeply in his relationship with God. As a student, he not only studied for his degree at UCSB, but he studied the Bible as well. As he grew in his understanding of God's love, he felt compelled to share his faith with others.

In the summer after his junior year, after raising his own financial support, Mike went on an international summer mission trip to East Asia. That summer, he was able to lead several students into a relationship with God. These students, having never heard of God or Jesus Christ, began to grow not only as new Christians but as spiritual leaders on their campuses.

Two years later, Mike returned to East Asia for a one-year STINT with Cru.[1] As Tim and his team, which consisted of college students and recent graduates, focused on evangelism and discipleship, God worked through them. Several Asian students came to faith in Christ and grew in their faith. However, Mike and his team had no idea of the seed they had planted.

Fast-forward fifteen years. The city in East Asia, where Mike visited and lived, now has a thriving campus ministry. There are spiritual movements at seven universities in the region. Thousands of college students have become Christians since Mike and his team went on their STINT, and many are missionaries themselves. A revival is happening in that country, a country that is closed to missionaries.

Mike's story is so compelling to me. I am amazed at how God used a young person to so radically advance his kingdom. God using a young person like Mike is nothing new. In fact, God has been using young men and women for thousands of years to help people know and grow in him.

JEREMIAH: BUT I'M JUST A KID!

I remember when I was a sophomore in high school and my youth pastor asked me to be a leader for a Mexico missions trip. It was the last thing I wanted to do.

But the next thing I knew, I was leading a team of other high school kids to help children in Tijuana, Mexico. I was terrified. I argued with my youth pastor. I argued with God. But I eventually gave in. I am so glad I did as God really worked in my life that week.

What if God asked you, as a young person, to tell the world about him? What if God called you to do something really crazy like go on a summer mission to help people know about Jesus? What if God asked you to share his love with your neighbor or family member? Well, it's not a matter of *if*. It's a matter of when! Would you be like me and argue out of fear and insecurity? Fortunately, we have several great examples in the Bible of young people who were asked by God to share his love with others.

God's Call and Jeremiah's Response

Jeremiah was born into and called to serve during an incredibly difficult time in history. At this point in the Bible, when the book of Jeremiah is written, God is fed up with the nation of Judah. These people participated in a number of evil practices such as human sacrifice and the worship of pagan gods. Their sin, wickedness, and constant turning from God were going to completely send them into ruin. Out of his love and grace, God wanted this nation to be saved from their wickedness. So God called Jeremiah to help this nation, these people, turn back to God. Jeremiah was asked to help a nation see their sin and renew their relationship with him.

That doesn't sound like a whole lot of fun, does it? It was a huge and challenging mission. In Jeremiah 1:4, God calls this young person to be a prophet to the nations, asking him to be a mouthpiece for him to the nation of Judah, saying, "Before I formed you in the womb I knew you, before you were born I set you apart; I appointed you as a prophet to the nations."

Jeremiah doesn't respond to God's call with immediate passion, courage, and excitement: This young man who eventually becomes a great leader responds with insecurity, excuses, and fear. He argues with God. I don't know about you, but I like that. I can relate! Let's look at two excuses Jeremiah uses when God calls him to share his love with others.

Excuse #1: I'm Too Young

"'Lord,' I said, 'I do not know how to speak; I am too young!'" (1:6). Jeremiah was indeed young: he was likely around seventeen years old when God called him to lead.

Yep, only seventeen years old.

When I was seventeen, I was thinking about what I was going to do with my buddies after school, where I was going to apply to college, and how I could convince a girl to go to the homecoming dance with me. I was hardly thinking of God using me to influence people to know him. But God wants to use all people, especially those of you who are young.

Excuse #2: I'm Too Inexperienced

Another excuse that Jeremiah gives is his lack of experience in "knowing how to speak." He complains to God that there is no way he could ever speak like a prophet (in those days, prophets were quite the public speakers). Jeremiah shows not just his uneasiness in following God's call but his insecurity in doing so. Jeremiah had no confidence that he could do what God was asking him to do.

Do you ever feel like that? Do you ever feel like God is calling you to do something, or to be something, that just seems too difficult? *The key thing to remember in this story of Jeremiah is not his response to God, but God's response to him.*

Response #1: Remember Who You Are

God responds to young Jeremiah's excuses with love and empowerment. First, look at how God approaches Jeremiah with such love and personal concern: "Now the word of the Lord came to me saying, before I formed you in the womb I knew you, and before you were born I consecrated you; I appointed you a prophet to the nations" (1:5). As God calls Jeremiah to this massive task of influencing a nation, he first reminds him of the standing he has before God. God reminds his child of the intimate and personal relationship they have. Think about it: The God of the universe is asking his child to do something significant and courageous, and he first reminds him of the love he has for him. It's as if God is saying, "Jeremiah, I knew all about this great calling on your life even before you were born. I set you apart for this time and this place."

Response #2: I Am With You

First, God responds to Jeremiah with love and care. Now look at what God says to Jeremiah after he hears another one of his excuses: "Then the Lord put out his hand and touched my mouth. And the Lord said to me, behold I have my put words in your mouth" (1:9). It's as if God looked at Jeremiah and said, "I've got your back on this; you can do it, Jeremiah. I am here to help you." And again, later in that first chapter, God reminds Jeremiah that he is with him and will deliver him.

I was on the swim team in high school. I remember getting ready to swim the 100-meter backstroke in the league finals. Many of my competitors had already beaten me that year in previous meets; they seemed twice my size, and I was swimming in their pool and in front of their crowd. As we jumped in the pool, my coach walked over, put his hand on my shoulder, and said,

"Shane, you've trained for this; you'll do great, and I'll be right here encouraging you through each turn and every stroke." This was the biggest race of my life and I jumped in the pool knowing my coach had my back. I was pretty sure I could have swum across the Pacific Ocean at that point. Thanks to the encouraging presence of my coach, I ended up winning that race.

God did something similar to Jeremiah. He empowered Jeremiah to do what he was called to do, something that was big and seemed impossible. That's how God operates. God never calls us to anything that we can't do without him. God calls us to do big things in influencing others to know and grow in him, as he did with Jeremiah. And just like with Jeremiah, when he calls us he's with us every step of the way.

We know the rest of the story, as Jeremiah does accept this challenge not only to influence the nation of Judah, but other nations as well. "A prophet to the nations, that's what I had in mind for you" (1:5). Jeremiah spoke of God's judgment and love to Egypt, Babylon, Edom, and Moab, as well as to Judah. It's amazing to me that this young man became a great leader who influenced beyond his own borders. As the *Bible Knowledge Commentary* explains: "Though Jeremiah proclaimed God's Word to Judah (chap. 2-45), his ministry as God's spokesperson extended beyond Judah to Gentile nations (chaps. 46-51)." [2] Jeremiah, though very hesitant at first, followed God's call and became known as a great leader in a very difficult time of history.

DAVID: THE REAL REASON HE KILLED THE GIANT

Most everyone knows the story of David: the shepherd boy who becomes king, the warrior child who literally cuts off the head of a nine-foot giant, the young man God chose to lead a nation, a man revered by many, a fruitful yet very flawed leader. From the first mention of David in the Bible, we see a young man who is utterly focused on his purpose: to make God's glory known throughout the earth.

I remember my Sunday school teacher in first grade sharing the story of David and Goliath. It gripped me as I thought of what it would be like to actually battle a warrior in front of thousands of people. Imagine an army on one side of a valley, another army on the other side, and two of their best soldiers squaring off in between. Except that the warrior representing the nation of Israel (God's army) is just a boy with no battle experience or training. The Philistines must think it's a cruel joke to present such a young Israelite to fight. When the two face one another—in front of everyone—a young and very bold David addresses his adversary:

> David said to the Philistine, "You come against me with sword and spear and javelin, but I come against you in the name of the Lord Almighty, the God of the armies of Israel, whom you have defied. This day the Lord will deliver you into my hands, and I'll strike you down and cut off your head. This very day I will give the carcasses of the Philistine army to the birds and the wild animals, and the whole world will know that there is a God in Israel. All those gathered here will know that it is not by sword or spear that the Lord saves; for the battle is the Lord's, and he will give all of you into our hands."
> 1 Samuel 17:45–47

Why was young David planning on slaying the giant? According to 1 Samuel, his reason was so that the whole world will know there is an extraordinary God in Israel.

David knew this incredible story would be heard by the world, and he wanted God to get credit for it. David knew the whole region would be talking of a young man defeating a giant, and the result would be God's name and glory displayed for the nations.

How old was David when he made such an impact? According to Bible scholars, David was just a teenager when he stepped out and defeated Goliath.

Throughout his life, David wrote for God's glory to be made known to the world. As stated, David knew his story of slaying Goliath would travel—and travel quickly—after their battle. David wanted to make sure God's fame, not his own, would be central to that story. David's passion to help the world know about God followed him throughout his life. I believe the book of

Psalms is the best book on missions ever written. Many Psalms that David wrote speak of God's glory being manifested to the nations.

There are many examples of David's writings in the Psalms that speak of God's glory spreading to the world: "All the ends of the earth will remember and turn to the Lord, and all the families of the nations will bow down before him, for dominion belongs to the Lord and he rules over the nations" (Psalm 22:27-28). Later, he writes, "All the nations you have made will come and worship before you, Lord; they will bring glory to your name. For you are great and do marvelous deeds; you alone are God" (Psalm 86:9-10). And we read of David's desire to have the nation of Israel bless the nations as God intended when he spoke to Abram in Genesis 12: "Sing to the LORD, all the earth; proclaim his salvation day after day. Declare his glory among the nations, his marvelous deeds among all peoples" (1 Chronicles 16:23-24). David was king of Israel for over forty years. From his battle with Goliath as a young man and throughout his life he spoke of God's desire to be known among the nations. [3]

Jeremiah and David are just two examples of people who God called to do big things. These young people—these world changers—live out courage and boldness, and even insecurity and fear, as they step out in faith and obey God. The examples continue throughout the Bible; we will look at two more in the following chapter.

QUESTIONS FOR INDIVIDUAL OR GROUP REFLECTION:

Describe a time of your life where you were asked to do something you thought impossible. Was there someone who came alongside you and encouraged you? What specifically did they do or say that helped you?

Does it surprise you that God chose two young people to write history? What impresses you most about Jeremiah?

How can you relate to the struggles Jeremiah faced as he stepped out in faith and followed God's call?

David writes throughout his life of God's desire to be known by all mankind. Reread Psalm 22:27-28 mentioned in this chapter. How do you think his battle with Goliath influenced his writings?

What was the most important takeaway from this chapter for you?

CHAPTER 3

A WOMAN AND A CHILD KING

"Without young men and women availing themselves to God, many of the great movements of Scripture and history would not have occurred."
Dan Hayes, *Fireseeds of Spiritual Awakening*

I recently heard from one of our students who was on STINT in the Middle East. She regularly meets with the president of the Muslim Student Association on one of the campuses there. Over the past semester they have become good friends and trust is being built.

This Muslim student said that she has been having a "dream jjabout the prophet Jesus visiting her." Our missionary told her friend that it is very special that Jesus would visit her in a dream. The Muslim girl responded that it actually isn't very special at all. It isn't special because she has thirteen friends in the Muslim Student Association on campus who have having the exact same dream.

It's actually not unusual for a Muslim to experience Jesus through a dream. I'm so glad that this girl, who recently graduated from college, was there to help her new friend know the real Jesus. She literally helped her interpret her dream! This is just one of many stories I hear of how God is working through young people around the world. It's awesome.

The worldwide spread of Christianity, in many ways, has been carried out by young people, especially college students or recent college graduates. We see this in the Bible and we see it in history.

I love the story of Charlotte "Lottie" Moon. Lottie is not widely recognized in missions circles, though she should be, as she has impacted the world like few others through her passionate commitment to spreading the reality of Jesus Christ to the nations. Lottie was raised on the East Coast of the United States and went to college in Virginia after the Civil War where she experienced a spiritual revival. Ironically, after this, she became known as someone who made fun of Christians on her college campus! A very educated woman, Lottie received one of the first Master of Arts degrees given to a woman in the South and she also spoke several languages. She "was a strong woman who lived an unusual life for her time." [4]

Lottie was driven to have an impact on people around the world for Jesus Christ like few others in her generation, man or woman. As a college student, Jesus Christ changed her life as "Lottie took away from school a new life and vision as a Christian. During a student revival in 1858, she went to a prayer meeting to scoff but left to pray all night." [5] Upon graduation from seminary, Lottie would settle for nothing less than sharing God's love with people around the world. She sailed for China to begin her career as a missionary at just twenty-three years old.

Right before leaving for China, she wrote, "Could a Christian woman possibly desire higher honor than to be permitted to go from house to house and tell of a savior to those who have never heard his name? We could not conceive life which would more thoroughly satisfy the mind and heart of a true follower of the Lord Jesus." [6]

Though a small woman, only four feet three inches tall, Lottie Moon has a large legacy. She died in 1912 and is revered by Christians around the world as one who committed herself to evangelism and global missions throughout her life.

JOSIAH: THE CHILD KING

In college I lived in the dorms. As I mentioned in the first chapter, I came across things that first year that were new choices for me as I was living on my own. Drinking anything from light beer to hard liquor, smoking pot, and watching pornography were a few options open to anyone on my floor at most any time of day.

To this day I thank God that I met Ethan.

Ethan was different and was not afraid to let those around him know why he was different. As a follower of Jesus he explained why he wouldn't participate in these activities, though he was also clear he was everyone's friend. I leaned on Ethan quite a bit that year. He not only made a difference in my own life in helping me say no to temptation and growing closer to God, but he made a significant impact on those around him in a very short period of time.

Kind of like a kid named Josiah.

King Josiah has only three and a half short chapters in the Old Testament, highlighting his reign of thirty-one years in Jerusalem and Judah. Yet in those chapters we see God use a young person to significantly influence a nation and bring reform. The Bible says that Josiah was a child when he began his reign: "Josiah was eight years old when he became king, and he reigned thirty-one years in Jerusalem" (2 Chronicles 34:1). After reigning for eight years, Josiah, at the age of sixteen, began to "seek the God of David his father, and in the twelfth year he began to purge Judah and Jerusalem of the high places" (2 Chronicles 34:3).

There is much significance to the reign of Josiah. Chapters 33 and 34 of 2 Chronicles highlight the reigns of Manasseh and Amon, the grandfather and father of Josiah, respectively. Manasseh was a wicked king – a bad dude, "and he did what was evil in the sight of the Lord, according to the abominations of the nations whom the Lord drove out before the people of Israel" (2 Chronicles 33:2). The son of Manasseh, who was assassinated, was evil as well: "Amon was twenty-two years old when he began to reign, and he reigned two years in Jerusalem. And he did what was evil in the sight of the Lord, as Manasseh his father had done" (2 Chronicles 33:22).

In just six years, God used Josiah to purify the practices of the nation of Israel and expand its borders and influence: "Josiah attempted a massive territorial expansion, including a reclaiming of the former northern kingdom beyond the northern limited regions already under Judean control." [7] As a youth, Josiah did not see his age as "an excuse or a handicap. As a young man, he had uninhibited freedom and energy, not burdened by responsibilities or worn down by years of shouldering them."[8]

As a teenager, Josiah pursued righteousness and purity, "and he did what was right in the ways of David his father, and he did not turn aside to the right hand or to the left" (2 Chronicles 34:2). As a result of his growing character and reliance on God, he took action with big results. God used him to implement radical change and a new commitment to God from Judah and Jerusalem. We read about this change in 2 Chronicles 34:29-32:

> Then the kings sent and gathered together all the elders of Judah and Jerusalem. And the king went up to the house of the Lord, with all the men of Judah and the inhabitants of Jerusalem and the priests and the Levites, all the people both great and small. And he read in their hearing all the words of the book of the Covenant that had been found in the house of the Lord. And the king stood in his place and made a covenant before the Lord, to walk after the Lord and keep his commandments and his testimonies and his statutes, with all his heart and with all his soul, to perform the words of the covenant that were written in this book. Then he made all who were present in Jerusalem and in Benjamin stand in it. And the inhabitants of Jerusalem did according to the covenant of God, the God of their fathers.

As a young person, Josiah made a serious impact in helping people, and an entire nation, follow God.

ESTHER: A YOUNG, ORPHANED, ETHNIC WOMAN

Imagine growing up without parents. What would it be like to grow up as an orphan with no mother or father? Now imagine, in Old Testament times, you were a woman growing up in a culture that constantly looked down on women and provided them little to no opportunity, especially compared to men. Now also imagine growing up in a culture where you were not only a woman, but also an ethnic minority. You were surrounded by a culture that was very different from yours, perhaps a culture that looked down on you.

Now imagine that young minority female orphan saving an entire race of people.

Now stop imagining. That really happened.

The Bible tells the story of a person just like the one above. Esther was a diaspora Jew living in Persia, an Israelite, who advanced God's mission in another land. The book of Esther is a classic rags-to-riches story.

As a review, the story of Esther is about a young and unknown woman chosen to become queen and eventually used by God to save the Jews. Esther was a young, ethnic minority living in a majority culture: the Persian Empire.

Early on in Esther, we are told that the king is looking for a wife, and one of the requirements he is looking for in a wife is youth: "And let the king appoint officers in all the provinces of his kingdom to gather all the beautiful young virgins to the harem in Susa the capital, under custody of Hegai, the king's eunuch, who is in charge of the women. Let the cosmetics be given to them. And let the young woman who pleases the king be queen instead of Vashti" (Esther 2:3-4).

The king eventually chooses Esther and this young woman develops as an influencer throughout the narrative; she grows throughout this story into a strong leader. Esther makes significant decisions and stands by them.

The story of Esther is of the advancement of the good news of God and his mission. Towards the end of the story of Esther, as a result of her actions and leadership, many people become followers of the one true God. [9] Scripture says, "The Jews had light and gladness and joy and honor. And in every province and in every city, wherever the king's command and his edict reached, there was gladness and joy among the Jews, a feast and a holiday. And many from the peoples of the country declared themselves Jews, for fear of the Jews had fallen on them" (Esther 8:16-17). The leadership of this young woman leads many to believe and practice the faith of the Jewish people. She brings salvation.

Esther advances God's mission. Esther also saves her people from certain death as she convinces the king to reverse the command given by Haman to kill the Jews:

> When the king held out the golden scepter to Esther, Esther rose and stood before the king. And she said, "If it please the king, and I have found favor in his sight, and if the thing seems right before the king, and if I am pleasing in his eyes, let an order be written to revoke the letters written by Haman the Agate, the son of Hammedatha, which he wrote to destroy the Jews who are in all the provinces of the king. For how can I bear to see the calamity that is coming to my people? Or how can I bear to see the destruction of my kindred?" Then King Ahasuerus said to Queen Esther and to Mordecai the Jew, "Behold, I have given Esther the house of Haman, and they have hanged him on the gallows, because he intended to lay hands on the Jews.
> Esther 8:4–8

Esther, in saving her people, paves the way for Jesus Christ, the coming Messiah. This story saves the Jewish people from certain death and even contradicts what the culture of the day thought of women in roles of influence. As author Drora Oren writes, "Esther, a Jewess, sentenced to die by Persian law, nonetheless shapes conceptions of what it is to be Persian. She not only brings salvation to a people destined for annihilation, but also questions the rigid alignments of Persian identity with male power." [10] God advances his mission of reaching out to the nations through the leadership and courage of this young, ethnic, orphaned woman.

Both Esther and Josiah show us that youth and other seeming disadvantages in life are hardly hindrances in sharing the reality of Jesus Christ. Now let's move on to the New Testament for even more stories of young people who changed the world.

QUESTIONS FOR INDIVIDUAL AND GROUP DISCUSSION

What about King Josiah is especially inspiring to you? Why? What surprised you as you read about his life?

What did you learn about Esther that you did not know before? What else is unique about the life of Esther?

Do you know someone, even if it's on a smaller scale, who makes an impact on people they way Josiah and Esther did?

CHAPTER 4

UNLIKELY LEADERSHIP: A PREGNANT TEENAGER

"Most of Jesus' disciples were in their mid-teens. Peter, having a family, may have been older – perhaps eighteen."
Leonard Sweet, *Jesus: A Theography*

William Cameron Townsend, a student at Occidental College in southern California in the early 1900s, heard of the need to distribute Christian literature in Central America. Before he graduated, he went for a summer to Guatemala to distribute Spanish-language Bibles. The problem Townsend encountered was eye-opening: many of the tribes did not even speak Spanish. A Kaqchiquel Indian even asked him, "If your God is so smart, why can't he speak my language?" [11] This college student eventually went on to establish Wycliffe Bible Translators and "resolved that every man, woman and child should be able to read God's Word in their own language." [12]

To date, Wycliffe has translated the Bible into well over 700 languages around the world. God used this young person to write down the Kaqchiquel language for the first time, translate the Bible for this tribe, build life-saving health centers, and eventually begin Wycliffe Bible Translators. This is yet another example of how God uses young people, and specifically college students, to influence the nations.

Isn't this crazy? Young people—*teenagers*—have been used by God throughout time to advance his kingdom. As the Old Testament is full of young people chosen to spread God's glory to the world, so is the New Testament. In this part of the Bible, we see Mary, the mother of Jesus; John Mark, who wrote the Gospel of Mark; and Timothy. They were all used as young people during the first century and whose influence extends even to today.

MARY

When discussing young people in the Bible who advanced God's mission, one person comes to the forefront for me: Mary, the mother of Jesus. Mary gave birth to Jesus when she was likely around fourteen to sixteen years old. This was not seen as too young for this culture at this time in history, as "Jewish females married around thirteen or fourteen years of age, males a little older." [13] God had a young woman bring the son of God into the world. My seminary professor and mentor, Dr. Leonard Sweet, speaks to this remarkable truth: "Consider this. When God decided to make His entrance upon this planet, He visited a woman. He chose a woman to bring forth the Eternal Son, the Messiah—the Anointed One for whom Israel had waited thousands of years. The life of God was placed in the womb of a woman before He got to you and to me. And God was not ashamed." [14] God chose a woman, a young woman, to initiate his plan of salvation for the world!

Mary was a change-agent. She was a revolutionary: "The Gospels come from many voices, and one of those was Mary's. Her voice tells us what God would do through her son to subvert the injustices of Herod and the pretentiousness of Augustus. Her voice told us that somehow, someway, someday, God would establish a kingdom of peace for the whole world."[15]

God used Mary to go against the traditional views the Jewish culture had towards women. For example, women were seen as property. They were not allowed to receive an education, and they were only allowed in certain parts of the home: the kitchen and the yard where the children played. Despite this, God used young Mary to bring his son into the world.

Mary was a true disciple of Jesus as she advanced his kingdom. Though not directly referred to as a disciple, Mary embodied a true follower and missionary of Jesus. Author and Reverend Father Betrand writes of Mary and her calling as a missionary:

> As a calling of Jesus, one is sent out to witness to him, to become a 'missionary', that is, to announce the Good News which is Jesus himself. According to Luke, in Acts of the

> Apostles, all disciples are believing Christians who are sent out to bring Jesus and his message to everyone. Matthew, too, tells us: 'Go therefore and make disciples of all the nations' (28:19). Discipleship becomes a universal call to holiness and witnessing to Jesus. [16]

The angel Gabriel told Mary that she would be the mother of the son of God: "The Holy Spirit will come upon you, and the power of the Most High will overshadow you; therefore the child to be born will be called holy—the Son of God" (Luke 1:35). As a disciple, Mary told others of Jesus. It's not a stretch to believe people had faith and followed him as a result. "Mary was a subversive and she was dangerous, first, because she knew the identity of her son and, second, because she began to tell his story." [17]

JOHN MARK

John Mark has always been held in the highest esteem in African Christianity. He was born in Africa, died in Africa, and is known to be the first person to bring the Gospel to this continent. Mark was not a direct disciple of Jesus, but was an early follower who obviously had great influence. Dr. William MacDonald writes, "As a young man, Mark and his mother joined the followers of Jesus. They became a part of a culture-transforming movement within Judaism. Later, Mark would be the first among the disciples to write the good news of the coming of this incomparable person who changed his life entirely." [18] Mark also wrote the oldest and shortest account (as a quick reader with a short attention span I appreciate this!) of the life of Jesus that is canonized in the New Testament, one which highlights the importance of servanthood and the reality of Jesus Christ. Though not as widely known, John Mark likely became a follower of Jesus through Peter, even traveling with him to share the Gospel. Dr. Thomas Oden writes, "[Mark] proceeded under Peter's guidance to the most southerly reach of the known world: Africa." [19]

There are instances in the gospel where we can arguably see Mark referred to as a young man. In Mark 14 we catch a glimpse of Mark, "A young man, wearing nothing but a linen garment, was following Jesus. When they seized him, he fled naked, leaving his garment behind" (Mark 14:51). Mark is the only writer to record this incident, which leads many to believe he is referring to himself. [20] A young man is again seen later in this gospel when "they looked up, they saw that the stone, which was very large, had been rolled away. As they entered the tomb, they saw a young man dressed in a white robe sitting on the right side, and they were alarmed" (Mark 16:4-5). We cannot say for sure that this is Mark, but many believe it is.

John Mark is mentioned several times in the rest of the New Testament, as he traveled with both Paul and Barnabas on their missionary journeys. Though Paul was obviously a missionary with great effectiveness, John Mark is known to have shared the good news of Jesus on *three* continents in his lifetime: Africa, Asia, and Europe.

Mark was a young man called to share the glory of God. His influence is still felt today, especially in Africa, with the world's fastest-growing Christian population. Africa has recently become a global force in Christianity and has more than 360 million Christians. With continuing growth over the next few decades, Africa will likely become the continent with the most Christians. This legacy began with a young man named John Mark.

TIMOTHY

Another young person the apostle Paul invested in was an inexperienced pastor named Timothy. Note that Paul, with all of his experience in leadership and education, chose Timothy, who was young and lacked a proven record of leadership, to mentor and help lead others to understand God. Paul did not choose a seasoned veteran or someone well known. Timothy's youth is referred to several times in both of Paul's letters to his friend, whom Paul called "son" or "child." Though Timothy's age is not given, we know he is young enough to be seen as inexperienced and perhaps even unqualified by some.

During my second year of college, I experienced spiritual

growth. I was involved in a college group at my church, and as a result, I was learning more and more about following Jesus. About halfway through the year, the pastor of that group asked if I would consider sharing my story with the group on a Sunday morning.

I was terrified.

The idea of standing in front of my peers, about one hundred of them, and talking about my relationship with God, was nerve-wracking! Speaking in front of any group was hardly something I wanted to do. In fact, I told my pastor I'd rather serve by cleaning the bathrooms. (He said he could arrange that, too.)

During that time, I was in a Bible study led by another student, Tim. Tim had been meeting with me over the previous year. Tim was a stud and a role model. He was a good leader. (And a really good surfer!)

On our way home from surfing one day, I shared with Tim what my pastor had asked me. He looked at me and said, "Shane, of course you are going to be nervous about this. Most anyone would be. But you're a leader and God wants to use your story to influence and lead others into a deeper relationship with him." His belief in me was all I needed.

Tim believed in me and it made all the difference as I considered standing in front of an audience to share my story.

The apostle Paul, known and revered throughout history for his boldness in evangelism, believed in Timothy. Though Paul empowered Timothy in God's mission, Timothy was not without fault: "As glowing a picture as the scripture paints of Timothy, it also includes his weaknesses as well. We find that he was young and intimidated." [21] Though he was young, Paul states in 1 Timothy that he has no doubt Timothy should be involved in teaching others about God, writing: "Don't let anyone look down on you because you are young, but set an example for the believers in speech, in conduct, in love, in faith and in purity" (1 Timothy 4:12). Youth did not impede Timothy from being involved in God's mission. Scripture does not imply that the apostle Paul chose Timothy because of his youth, but we do know it did not stop him from believing that Timothy could be an effective evangelist. Remember, friends, your youth does not mean you can't be fruitful as you share the reality of Jesus Christ with those around you! As we've read, God has used young people in incredible and crazy ways to grow his kingdom.

Mary, John Mark, and Timothy are three examples of young people used in advancing the mission of God in the New Testament, and their influence has been felt for over two thousand years. They are three young people in a long line of youth throughout the Bible, both in the Old and New Testaments, who are pivotal in advancing God's mission of glorifying himself among all nations and all peoples.

QUESTIONS FOR INDIVIDUAL OR GROUP REFLECTION

Mary, Mark, and Timothy are among many young people who advanced God's kingdom throughout the Bible. Find other young people that God used and discuss them together.

As you read about Mary, Mark, and Timothy what qualities stand out to you the most? Why?

Who in your life has some of these qualities? How do they live them out?

CHAPTER 5

YOUTH GOING BIG

"Nearly every major mission movement in modern history had college-age young people at the forefront. Then and now, they supply the crucial personnel for the bottle-necked task of which Jesus spoke in Matthew 9, 'The harvest is plentiful, but the laborers are few.'"
Steve Shadrach

"It is remarkable that students have played a decisive role in many of the greatest forward movements of the church in world evangelism. It has been through their vision and energy that the church has been propelled into renewed efforts of outreach." [22]
David Howard, MissionsFrontiers.org

My family and I recently lived in Puerto Rico on STINT. I remember going to a campus right after we moved there and meeting a student named Juan-Carlos. Juan-Carlos filled out a survey for me about spirituality. As I spoke with him about his religious background and his life story, I asked him if he would have thirty minutes to talk about what it means to have a relationship with God through the person of Jesus Christ. I remember thinking, "This kid doesn't want to talk to me and he doesn't want to talk about Jesus."

I was wrong.

After an hour of conversation, Juan-Carlos prayed and became a follower of Jesus, right there in the cafeteria on campus. Since that time, Juan-Carlos has brought his friends to church, prays for his friends on a daily basis, and has seen one of his friends come into a relationship with Jesus. I was recently with Juan-Carlos's parents and they told me that their son has become a model to them as he walks with Jesus.

Young people like Juan-Carlos have always influenced their friends and peers in a way that brings them to Christ. History shows this throughout the Bible and throughout the last two millennia as well.

This chapter explores the early origins of the worldwide global missions movement that began in the early 4th century and continued through the 18th century. This history lesson goes quick, so hold on.

THE 4TH AND 5TH CENTURIES

In the early centuries of Christianity, the missionary zeal of the church decreased, and missionary expansion did not increase significantly until after the 16th century. [23] Much has been written about why this is the case and how the church expanded (though little) before the year 1700. [24] The purpose of this chapter is to show how university students have contributed to the global expansion of Christianity, but I think it's important to share a bit about a slave who impacted the world hundreds of years even before the university was established. Though little happened in the way of missions early on, one person who advanced the Gospel in this time stands out: Saint Patrick.

Though born into a Christian family, Patrick did not embrace the Christian faith. When he was only sixteen years old, Patrick was kidnapped from his home in Northeast England and taken by pirates to Ireland. His captors put Patrick to work herding cattle. In just a few years, Patrick became a Christian. As a result of his conversion on the hills of Ireland, young Patrick grew to love his God and his captors:

> Patrick changed in another way during the periods he spent with his captors in their settlement. He came to understand the Irish Celtic people, and their language and culture, with the kind of intuitive profundity that is usually possible only, as in Patrick's case, from the underside. Patrick came to love his captors, to identify with them, and to hope for their

> reconciliation with God. One day he would feel they were his people.[25]

At the age of twenty-two, Patrick had a vision that would change his life and eventually the lives of the Celtic people. In his vision, Patrick was prompted to run to the coast and escape on a ship back to England. Later, but still as a young man, Patrick trained to become a priest and then had another vision. Patrick sensed God calling him back to the Celtic people, his former captors, to give them an opportunity to hear about Christianity. Patrick had little to no model for this mission because there had been no previous outreach by the church to the "barbarians" (what non-believers were referred to in those days) in the early centuries. Despite this fact, Patrick set sail back to Ireland.

Patrick's spiritual influence on Ireland, and the world, is remarkable. As Dr. Hunter writes,

> The Celtic Christian Movement proceeded to multiply mission-sending monastic communities, which continued to send teams into settlements to multiply churches and start people in the community-based life of full devotion to God. In two or three generations, all of Ireland had become substantially Christian and Celtic monastic communities became the strategic "missions stations" from which apostolic bands reached the "barbarians" of Scotland, and much of England, and much of Western Europe.[26]

Patrick had studied throughout his twenties and thirties in preparation to go back to Ireland. After arriving, he contextualized his faith by becoming like those he was hoping to reach, providing a model for how to best reach other cultures for Jesus Christ. Patrick was not a youth when he set out to evangelize Ireland. However, he was a youth—your age—when he sensed God call him into ministry, which eventually led him back to plant and grow Christian communities where he was once a prisoner.

THE DARK AND MIDDLE AGES

Young people, even before the traditional university was founded, were making an impact in the expansion of Christianity around the world. The cultural and intellectual centers in the Dark and Middle Ages were the monasteries. Monasteries were sending out the missionaries and the church planters to spread the gospel. The scholar Boniface (680-754) was an English monk who was also known as an evangelist and missionary. Martin of Tours, a French monk, traveled for most of his life spreading Christianity. And Columba (521-597) founded an Irish monastery that was known as the center for evangelization throughout his country. Though there were no university students *per se*, the academic centers of the times were sending missionaries and evangelists to expand Christianity around the world.

KEY PLAYERS

Count Nikolas Ludwig von Zinzendorf

Count Nikolas was born in 1700 in Dresden, Germany. His brief sixty years of life left a mark on the history of missions like few others. Count Nikolas has become known as one of the most influential evangelists and missionaries in history. Dr. Ruth Tucker, professor of missiology at Calvin Theological Seminary, writes of his influence: "He pioneered ecumenical evangelism, founded the Moravian church, and authored scores of hymns; but above all else, he launched a worldwide missionary movement that set the stage for William Carey and the 'Great Century' of missions that would follow." [27]

Count Nikolas, a bright and privileged child, was sent to the Halle Pietist boarding school at the age of ten. As a young person, he grew in his understanding of God and his love for him. This led to him initiating a campus club, at the age of just sixteen, that would later be called "The Order of the Grain of Mustard Seed." Imagine using that name for your new Bible study group on your campus; it would certainly take up a lot of space on your Facebook page!

Remember we are talking about students here, not professionally trained pastors, not students in seminary, not teachers of the Bible. Don't get me wrong, professionals are very important; I have several graduate degrees myself. The point I'm making is that these are young college students who stepped out in faith and believed God.

The mission of this group of students led by Count Nikolas was simply to grow in their love for God and to grow in their love for people. He began this club with one of his best friends, another student named John de Watteville. "The two sixteen-year-olds pledged that they each would do all in their power to carry the message concerning Jesus Christ to all people, but especially to those to whom no one else would go, or about whom no one else cared. This pledge would later be carried out in outstanding fashion." [28]

Count Nikolas graduated as the valedictorian of his class in 1716, only sixteen years old, and left to begin his study of law at the University of Wittenberg. His commitment to Jesus Christ and to study the Bible followed him throughout his university career, as did his devotion to reach the world for Jesus Christ. He and the members of his fraternity, now established at the University of Wittenberg, were intent to make Jesus Christ known everywhere. Their commitment as eager students to impact the world was obvious to everyone: "To the members of the Order of the Mustard Seed, every follower of Christ was a missionary, whether at home or in the farthest corners of the earth. Thus, Zinzendorf and de Watteville were not only committed to sending others overseas, but they were equally determined to spread the gospel in whatever context they found themselves." [29] It's so impressive to me that this commitment to mission was coming from teenage students.

The accomplishments and influence he had in the context of missions and the church is remarkable–it really is amazing. After graduating and beginning his career as an attorney, Count Nikolas purchased a large piece of property. Within a year, several hundred persecuted congregants from the United Brethren Church gathered on his land and asked permission to stay. He welcomed them and others began to join this group.

This small group of people, who were known as Moravians, had a passion to pray. In 1727, forty-eight of these Christians began a twenty-four-hour prayer chain. This prayer chain lasted one hundred years.

Yes, you read that correctly: a prayer chain lasting one hundred years.

As a result of this prayer movement, Count Nikolas and his flock grew in their commitment to evangelize the world for Jesus Christ. This small band of Christians took Jesus' words of multiplication very seriously: "All authority in heaven and earth has been given to me. Go therefore and make disciples of all nations, baptizing them in the name of the Father and of the Son and of the Holy Spirit, teaching them to observe all that I have commanded you. And behold, I am with you always, even to the end of the age" (Matthew 28:18-20). In 1732, the Moravians sent their first missionaries: Leonard Dober and David Nitschmann. These men travelled to St. Thomas in the West Indies to evangelize slaves. This was the beginning of an incredible missionary-sending effort by the Moravians that would spread to Algeria, Jamaica, Greenland, North America, several countries in Africa, and throughout Romania. From this incredible sending effort, Count Nikolas is referred to as the "Father of Modern Missions."

Around the time of Count Nikolas, other young people were advancing the Gospel as well. The well-known Wesley brothers, John and Charles, met a group of Moravians in 1736 aboard a ship sailing to North America. In the middle of a great storm, when both Wesleys thought their ship was sinking, they noticed the peace and faith the Moravians displayed in the chaos of the wind and waves. Dr. Leonard Sweet writes of the profound impact the Moravians had on the Wesleys:

> The Wesleys first discovered the power of the congregational hymn singing while on a voyage with twenty-six German Moravians to Georgia in 1735. It wasn't the storm that shook [John] Wesley's heart and turned it inside out. Granted the storm was scary enough. It split the windjammer's mainsail and broke the mast in two. Passengers were running hither and yon, scrambling for cover–except for the Moravians.

> They calmly kept singing. The stronger the winds howled, the louder they sang; and the louder they sang, the stronger their faith. What so moved Wesley was not the fierceness of the storm, but the singing in the storm. Not the song in the storm, but their singing in the storm is what drew him to a deeper faith. Later, at a Moravian meetinghouse in London, he would give himself fully to Jesus. [30]

The impact John Wesley had made by the time of his death is amazing. As author Alice Russie explains, "At the time of his death, there were eighty thousand members of the societies under his care; three hundred itinerant and one thousand local preachers; eight mission stations in the West Indies, and eight in British America. After his death, these societies became the backbone of the infant Methodist Church." [31] The Wesley brothers are known as theologians and pastors who contributed to the first Great Awakening, Methodism, and many people coming to faith in Jesus Christ. As young men, they began their ministries as missionaries. By the end of his life, Charles Wesley had written over 8,000 hymns. His brother John delivered over 40,000 sermons in his lifetime and rode over 250,000 miles on horseback preaching the gospel. Their spiritual heritage can be traced back to the Moravians and young Count Nikolas.

Count Nikolas died in 1760 with his best friend (from his youth) and co-founder of the Order of the Grain of the Mustard Seed, John de Watteville, by his side. When he died, his Moravian movement had sent out more missionaries overseas in twenty years than Protestants and Anglicans had done in the previous two centuries.

Samuel Mills

Another young person of influence in the early years of modern missions, and in sending college students to evangelize the world, was Samuel Mills. [32] Mills became a Christian when he was seventeen and entered Williams College in 1806. Mills was hardly anything to look at: "he was unattractive intellectually and physically." [33] He definitely lacked stage presence and charisma: "As an incoming freshman at Williams College, friends of Samuel Mills described him as a tall, quirky guy with a squeaky voice." [34]

He may have had his awkward social moments, but Mills was passionate and mobilized students to go evangelize the world. Mills participated in a prayer gathering on campus every Wednesday and Friday afternoon at Williams College. He was especially passionate about Jesus' words in praying for laborers in Matthew 9:37-38: "The harvest is plentiful, but the laborers are few; therefore pray earnestly to the Lord of the harvest to send out laborers to his harvest." One Saturday afternoon while Mills was leading a time of prayer and Bible study, it began to rain. Mills and four other students scrambled for shelter under a haystack and held the prayer meeting there. In this particular time of prayer, they asked God to reach Asia, and they prayed for other university students to go to Asia as missionaries. This event, "a landmark in American Foreign Missions," [35] became known as the "Haystack Prayer Meeting." This meeting has become widely recognized as the catalyst of the first era of missions.

These five students were eventually the first five American university students to go overseas as missionaries. This group of students would go on to begin the American Board of Commissioners for Foreign Missions, the first missionary-sending agency in the United States. Samuel Mills also "led in the formation of the American Board of Commissioners for Foreign Missions, the American Bible Society, the United Foreign Missions Society, and other benevolent organizations." [36]

Samuel Mills, after attending seminary, eventually set sail for Africa in 1817 with a dream of freeing the slaves and sending them into their own continent as missionaries to Africa. Just one year later, and only twelve years after that historic prayer meeting under the haystack, Samuel Mills died. He is now known as the father of foreign mission work in America. The missionary movement in the United States traces its beginnings back to that prayer meeting, initiated by a young university student at Williams College.

Charles Simeon

Charles Simeon came to know Jesus Christ as a college student in 1779 at Cambridge University. He entered as a non-believer and graduated a Christian. After he became a follower of Jesus, he could do nothing less than set his eyes on the things of Christ. He lived out the Apostle Paul's challenge to the church in Colossae: "If then you have been raised up with Christ, seek the things that are above, where Christ is, seated at the right hand of God. Set your minds on things that are above, not on things that are on earth. For you have died, and your life is hidden with Christ in God" (Colossians 3:1-2). Simeon left a lasting influence that was felt in England and around the world. Upon graduation, he went straight into the ministry. "Students who came under Simeon's influence in Cambridge later became some of the great leaders of the church both in Great Britain and around the world." [37]

D.L. Moody, the American evangelist, came across the Atlantic Ocean to visit Simeon and to proclaim the gospel to students at Cambridge University. Moody's impact on this campus and many campuses here in America was instrumental in the growth of the Student Volunteer Movement (SVM). Many students were converted to Christianity and were mobilized for world missions as a result of the SVM. About this time, seven students on Simeon's campus applied to Hudson Taylor's China Inland Mission and later went as missionaries to China. Their impact was tremendous: "In February 1885, the seven sailed for China, to be followed in subsequent years by scores of students, who under their influence, had given themselves to Jesus Christ to reach other parts of the world that still awaited the gospel." [38] Under Simeon's leadership, God raised up an army of students to reach the world.

These are just a few examples—I could write of dozens more—of young people who prayed, stepped out in faith as God called them, and led in initiating missions around the world. I say it all the time: God has always used young people to advance his kingdom. He has always used these world changers to bring people into his kingdom. Why wouldn't he continue to work in this way?

Why wouldn't he use you?

QUESTIONS FOR INDIVIDUAL AND GROUP REFLECTION

St. Patrick had a vision from God to become a missionary. What do you think he wrestled with as he considered going back to the very people that enslaved him?

Many of these young people, including Charles Simeon, became followers of Jesus as students. They then went to the mission field right after college. Does this surprise you? If so, why?

I love that Count Nikolas was involved in missions and evangelism with his best friend, John de Watteville, for his entire life. Watteville was even present when Zinzendorf left this life for the next. Who are good friends you could see being on mission with for your lifetime?

CHAPTER 6

EVEN BIGGER

"The object of this Society shall be the cultivation of a missionary spirit among the students of the College, the information of its members in all subjects of missionary interest, and especially the leading men to consecrate themselves to foreign missionary work... Any student of the College who is a professing Christian may become a member by subscribing to the following covenant: We, the undersigned, declare ourselves willing and desirous, God permitting, to go to the unevangelized portions of the world." [39]
Student Robert Wilder, Princeton College, 1883

As I've mentioned earlier, I love to surf. Recently, a guy asked me during a surf session why I was studying to receive my doctorate. He was curious as to why I was putting the time and money into a degree that would not gain me greater title or compensation. He is not a follower of Jesus (well, not yet, anyway) and was quite curious about what I was doing.

I told him that was easy to answer. But then a really good wave came and I had to take it. (When a good wave comes you just have to go.) When I saw him later we continued our conversation. As we shared waves, I told him, "Young people have always led in global missions. History points to young people being in the middle of sharing the reality of Jesus Christ with cultures around the world. I want to learn more about these world changers, and to know how to better empower and send them."

He had no idea how to respond.

That's okay, and I thought, *"Hey buddy, you asked me, so I answered you."*

GRACE AND ROBERT WILDER

I love the story of a young leader named Grace Wilder. Wilder is yet another university student who has significantly advanced evangelism around the world. Wilder was raised in India in a missionary home and then educated in America. During her time as a college student, she attended Mount Holyoke College in Massachusetts and influenced others to go into missions. She led a Bible study on campus where women had to sign a missionary pledge to be a member. She was also known as a person of prayer, consistently asking God to send students to evangelize the nations. She was instrumental in the growth of the Student Volunteer Movement, a key organization that mobilized student missions from America to go abroad. Author Jessica Ahrend writes, "We should not forget that God redeemed His promise of answering prayer, and this was the faithful and effectual prayer of Miss Wilder and her brother, which, humanly speaking, began this work." [40]

After her graduation, Grace returned to Princeton to help care for her sick father and it was during this season (1885-1886) that she and her and her brother and a handful of others saturated the nights with prayer. They begged God that a widespread missionary movement would sweep through the colleges and universities of America. They agreed together and asked God to raise up 1,000 volunteers that would go from the universities to the foreign mission field. During these countless hours that Grace, Robert, and their peers spent on their knees, the revival of missionary zeal, soon to become the Student Volunteer Movement, was born. [41]

At the age of twenty-six, Wilder was sent by the Presbyterian Board to India. During her time spent on furlough back in America, she was determined to mobilize more students to go as missionaries to India: "During her furlough she spent time on college campuses speaking to and mobilizing female students to India." [42] The result was fruitful as she continued to invest her life in students. When Wilder returned to India, she brought five women with her to share the gospel. "She died in 1911 at age fifty, having given her life to mobilizing students and evangelizing the unreached."[43]

Grace's brother, Robert P. Wilder, also played a significant role as a student who mobilized other students to share their faith. As a student at Princeton College in 1883, Wilder attended a conference with two of his friends and was challenged as a result of it. "We three college students returned to Princeton inspired with the desire to accomplish two things. First, to pray and work for revival in our college, and second, to stir up missionary interest. We prevailed on like-minded students to form groups, usually consisting of three or four, who met daily."[44] Robert and his sister Grace were passionate about praying and consistently met "to pray for a wide-spread missionary movement in the colleges and universities of America. We asked that ultimately one thousand volunteers might be secured to labor in foreign fields."[45]

Robert attended a conference that challenged him to mobilize other university students for foreign missionary service.[46] Wilder, with a group of four other students, committed to taking the following year to travel from university to university challenging students to go as missionaries to the world. His four friends at the last moment decided to back out of their commitment (for many of the same reasons students face today). Wilder decided to go on his own and at the last minute another student, John Forman, joined him on his travels. The tour of universities the following year resulted in 2,106 student volunteers from 162 colleges signing a pledge to go into foreign missionary service. Five hundred and fifty women joined the cause as well. That year, Wilder spoke at Hope College. In attendance was Samuel Zwemer who, along with several classmates, volunteered for missionary service overseas and is "sometimes referred to as the 'Apostle to Islam.' Zwemer more than anyone else put the Muslim world on the map."[47]

Robert Wilder would eventually become one of the key leaders of the Student Volunteer Movement. I love this letter from student missionaries whom he mobilized and how it demonstrates his impact:

> Dear Mr. Wilder,
> Last Sunday afternoon, on board the Empress of Russia,

> bound for the Orient, over fifty men and women held a meeting in the name of the Student Volunteer Movement. Most of them were Student Volunteers. We want you to know first, that we love the SVM. We love it because of what it meant and continues to mean to us. We love it because of the friendships made under its auspices which reach out to all parts of the world. We love it because we love Him who serves.
>
> Then, we want you to know we believe in it. We believe in its ideals and policies, its plans and purposes. We believe in its living Watchword—"The Evangelization of the World in This Generation." We believe in those who are directing its activities—you as General Secretary, the Executive Committee, the Council and the Secretaries. We believe in all its possibilities for good led by the Spirit of God.And finally, we want you to know it is our desire and purpose to support the Movement by our thought and our prayers and our gifts. We are still Student Volunteers. The Movement is still our Movement. Count on us always. May the Lord greatly and richly bless the work of the Movement this school year in all the colleges and universities. [48]

C.T. STUDD AND THE CAMBRIDGE SEVEN

C.T. Studd was born in England in 1860. Upon entering Cambridge University, he became well known for his ability as a cricket player and captained the team as a student.

Even today, Studd is revered as one of the best cricket players in history. As a student-athlete at Cambridge, Studd (isn't that a great name?) was also part of a Bible study that met on campus. The primary focus of this group was to promote the evangelization of the world. As Studd and his friends shared Jesus Christ with their peers at Cambridge, they also begin to challenge students to share God's love with the rest of the world. This group of friends eventually became known as "The Cambridge Seven." This group's passion was to pray for and mobilize students to go to China in the name of Jesus Christ.

When he graduated, Studd walked away from a professional career as a cricket player to become a missionary to China. Imagine the winner of the Heisman trophy turning down a professional football career. That's what Studd did. Though his parents were against the idea of him becoming a missionary, he was going anyway. Before setting sail, Studd and these other young men traveled across England visiting universities and challenging students to join them. They spent an entire year meeting with and mobilizing other university students to go overseas to point others to Jesus. After a fruitful year of mobilizing other students, the Cambridge Seven left for China in 1885.

Studd died in 1900. He widely influenced missions in China, India, and Africa. Studd influenced his brother in missions as well. J.E.K. Studd spoke at Cornell University in 1897 challenging students to go to the mission field. One student, John Mott, heard him and even met with Studd the following day. John Mott would come to lead the Student Volunteer Movement.

JOHN MOTT

John Mott was born on May 25, 1865. Raised in a Christian home, Mott became a follower of Jesus Christ as a young man. When he was only sixteen, he entered college at Upper Iowa University and in 1885 transferred to Cornell University. It was at Cornell where Mott's life was changed. Mott's leadership as a student and throughout his life would impact the Church like few others. I love this quote, written after his death, that demonstrates his life's impact:

> The contrast between the Christian enterprise as it was in 1888, when John R. Mott graduated from college, and as it is today is as striking between the political world of that time and the present. And at nearly every moment of decision in the church history of these revolutionary years, when new directions were to be attempted or new dimensions of effort embraced, the leader who made all the difference was this

> American layman, John R. Mott.[49]

This meeting led Mott to attend a camp held in Mt. Hermon, Massachusetts for college students from almost ninety universities. During this four-week Bible and missions conference, a student from Princeton University, Robert Wilder, the brother of Grace Wilder, challenged his peers to sign a pledge that would commit them to missionary service overseas. Mott signed this pledge alongside ninety-nine other students. This group of students would come to be known as the "Mount Hermon Hundred."

THE STUDENT VOLUNTEER MOVEMENT

These one hundred students would mark the beginning of the Student Volunteer Movement for Foreign Missions. Mott would become the leader of this movement. Mott's purpose as he led the SVM was to mobilize university students to go to the world with the reality of Jesus Christ. Mott traveled throughout the United States and the world his entire life, challenging and mobilizing young people to go into foreign missions. Mott and his leadership of the SVM resulted in a new momentum of missionaries going to the field:

> By 1870 America had sent out a total of only about 2,000 Protestant missionaries, and by 1890 there were only 934 American foreign missionaries in the field, a feeble effort for a nation with the population, wealth and pretensions that America had in the nineteenth century. By the turn of the century, however, there were 5,000 American missionaries, by 1915 there were 9,000 and by the end of the 1920s there were 14,000. The transition from anemic if nominal efforts to a determined and concerted program to evangelize the world occurred in the last quarter of the century and blossomed in the last decade of that century through a variety of new organizations, the most influential being the Student Volunteer Movement for Foreign Missions.[50]

It's just amazing to see the momentum the SVM created in sending missionaries to foreign service, with the vast majority of those sent being challenged when they were college students. "The distinct purpose of the Student Volunteer Movement is to secure student volunteers who will actually go forth from the United States and Canada to spend their lives in non-Christian lands and the work of establishing Christ's Kingdom." [51] Students heard the rally cry of the SVM under Mott's leadership,

> The long continued cry of the Church, "Whom shall we send—who will go for us?" has given place to the answering cry of the college world, "We will go, but who will send us?" Her prayers to the Lord of the harvest have been answered by a multitude of the choicest young men and women, who with the enthusiasm begotten of youth, and also impelled, as we believe, by the Holy Spirit, are eagerly entreating to be sent forth into His harvest... The first general response of the student volunteers, therefore, rang with cheerful confidence. It was brief, hearty, positive, triumphant. It was simply, "We will go." [52]

The purpose of the SVM obviously resonated with students, and under Mott's leadership, the movement spurred an awakening in missionary sending like nothing seen in history:

> As a result of this program, the movement enrolled, between 1886 and 1936, just under 50,000 student volunteers, of which number over 13,000 actually sailed to the foreign fields of missionary service. These workers served either under the Church boards or under some form of interdenominational agency related to the churches. During this fifty-year period approximately half of the missionaries sent out were Student Volunteers. The peek was in 1908 when two-thirds of the missionaries appointed were members of the Movement. [53]

Mott did more than just mobilize university students for missionary service throughout his lifetime. He also authored sixteen books, many on the importance of being involved in evangelism around the world. Mott was asked by President Woodrow Wilson three times to become the ambassador to China; he declined, each time citing the importance of world evangelization as his reason not to take the role. He was awarded the Distinguished Service Medal by Congress and was asked to lead five educational institutions, including Yale and Princeton. Mott traveled across the Atlantic Ocean over one hundred times and the Pacific Ocean fourteen times and received six honorary degrees. Mott facilitated the Edinburgh Missionary Conference, the first ever interdenominational missionary conference.

Mott also organized the World Student Christian Federation that grew to include campus clubs, or "societies," on over three thousand universities around the world. In 1946, Mott received the Nobel Peace Prize. He was married for sixty-two years and continued to travel and speak to students about world evangelism even after his wife's death.

QUESTIONS FOR INDIVIDUAL AND GROUP REFLECTION

What resonates with you most about Robert and Grace Wilder, John Mott, and C.T. Studd? Why?

Many of these young missionaries were challenged to go to the world at a conference, Mount Hermon. Have you ever been to a camp or conference that challenged you in a similar way?

As we see the pattern of God using young people throughout time to spread the Gospel, what qualities do these young people have in common?

CHAPTER 7

SHOW ME THE MONEY: THE DANGERS OF DEBT

"The average university graduate leaves college with a $24,000 weight around their neck: student loans. This keeps many recent grads from considering overseas service."
Josh Cooper, *Hold Fast: The Mission of God and the Obstacles of Man*

> Those who love money will never have enough.
> Ecclesiastes 5:10

> Let no debt remain outstanding, except the continuing debt to love one another. Romans 13:8

As he received his diploma and walked off stage, Kai was ready to make an impact, to influence, and to help others see how God is working around them. As a student at the University of Arizona, Kai learned about Jesus Christ from his R.A. His sophomore year, he led a Bible study of freshmen in a dorm, and as a junior he participated in a stateside summer mission trip where he learned how to share his faith. During his junior and senior years, Kai interned in a local accounting firm near campus, gaining experience and reaching out to people in the workplace.

His senior year, Kai learned more about God's heart for the world and God's plan to reach the world. Kai spent a week in the Middle East with Cru on a vision trip interacting with Muslim students. Kai was amazed at the number of students who had never heard about Jesus in this 10/40 window country. The 10/40 window (10 degrees north and 40 degrees north latitude) represents where the majority of the world's unreached people groups live. As he prepared to leave after only ten days, a Muslim student said to Kai, "Thank you for being my friend, thank you for telling me about Jesus." Kai told his Arab friend that he hoped to be back one day to continue to share with him.

Six months later, Kai was living at home, struggling to find a job, and not even considering becoming a missionary. This once passionate and eager young person wondered if he would ever have an opportunity to share his faith in a cross-cultural setting again.

Kai's story is heartbreaking, isn't it? Kai is in debt, both with several credit cards and school loans.

An obvious and significant hurdle for students who want to go to the mission field is in the area of finances. Years ago as a student, I remember walking on campus as a freshman and having ample opportunities to fill out credit-card applications. Visa, American Express, Discover, and MasterCard were desperately trying to gain me as a friend and customer. Today is no different. These companies target students from day one, as it's not uncommon to see tables set up on campuses promoting credit card companies. [54] The statistics are staggering. According to `credit.com`, the average undergraduate student currently has $3,100 of credit card debt and will graduate with over $4,000 of credit card debt. Add to this the fact that students graduate with an average of more than $25,000 of school loans, and we see how finances weigh on college students as they are enslaved to repay large loans. According to the website, young people typically spend approximately one-third of their income on debt repayment.

Author and speaker Josh Cooper has been traveling around the United States speaking at conferences, churches, and universities mobilizing students for missions for the past three years. Cooper says that debt is one of the biggest obstacles a college student faces when considering missions:

> The majority of people walk a fine line regarding debt. For Christians the stakes are high. It is a major obstacle to fulfilling the Great Commission. It affects how much we give and whether we are free to go. I'm not able to step out in faith when I am miles deep in debt. It can sideline you from

> ministry. It's an issue for anyone desiring to play a role in world evangelization, regardless of geography or vocation. [55]

Look at these following statistics taken from American Student Assistance, a non-profit focusing on helping students with loan solutions: [56]

1. Students graduate with an average of $27,000 of school loans.
2. There is $1 trillion in outstanding student loan debt in the United States.
3. 66% of students graduate with education debt.
4. Only 26% of students graduate with no debt.
5. Borrowers under 30 years old total $292 billion in education debt.
6. Two of five student loan borrowers are delinquent within five years of graduation.

Credit-card debt combined with student-loan debt is a burden for graduating students. Students who graduate and enter the workplace soon begin to pay a significant amount of their earnings to their debts. Dr. Lillian Guerra of Yale University writes of her own experience with debt:

> As a graduate of Dartmouth College who holds a Ph.D. from the University of Wisconsin-Madison, I launched my academic career with a total debt load of over $105,000. As soon as I started working as a full-time faculty member six years ago, I began to make payments of between $600 and $1,000 a month to creditors, depending on what my current salary was. Let me be clear: my current salary would be terrific if one third of it was not going to such creditors as the U.S. Department of Education. [57]

Later on in her article, Dr. Guerra writes of many students now taking nine or even ten years to complete their graduate degrees because of the burden of debt.

In a recent interview with a young missionary from California Polytechnic University in Pomona, I asked, "What is one of the biggest obstacles you and others have when considering overseas missions?"

Her answer was straightforward and to the point: "Debt; students graduate with school loans and credit-card debt and they are really only able to think of how to pay down their massive amounts of debt."

As I travel to campuses around the country, I'm actually surprised when I speak with students who graduate with *no debt*, including credit-card debt. When I am asking students to prayerfully consider going to the mission field for a summer or for a year, I often hear of finances being the barrier holding them back.

I think of a young friend of mine named Nathan. Nathan was an outstanding student. He was involved in sports (he was on the swim team in college and even found time to surf with me quite a bit), a fraternity, had a part-time job, and even co-led a Bible study in a freshmen dorm. He mentored young guys on campus and spent time with international students. Upon graduation, he wanted to do something incredible with his life—he wanted to be a missionary. One thing stood in his way: Over $45,000 in student loans. One finance expert saw this with a previous client: "I have known people who have not been able to go to the mission field because of debt. Going is their intention, but unfortunately life happens. They start off working hard to get the loan paid off, but end up with obligations and ties as time rolls on." [58]

As a missions mobilizer, this is devastating for me to see. I have met and interacted with too many young people who desire to go to the mission field but are held back due to financial concerns.

CONFRONTING DEBT AND UNDERSTANDING GOD'S VIEW OF FINANCES

The Bible has much to say about money and our personal finances. Money is mentioned over 2,000 times in the Bible, more than faith and prayer combined! Unfortunately, many college students and young people are not aware of God's concern with our finances and his simple and helpful instructions in how we steward them.

I remember a conversation I had with a student at UC Santa Barbara several years ago. My friend was anxious about the debt he was incurring with his student loans. Upon graduation he would have started paying back approximately $60,000. He was incurring $15,000 a year to go to school, which at that time was a good amount. He told me he regretted not attending a junior college the first few years to take the same courses and keep his costs down. I asked him why he didn't. His answer? "I don't know, I just didn't really think about it."

Take a minute right now and think about it.

How much credit card and school debt do you have? How much do you think you will incur over the next several years? How can you avoid most of that debt?

Let me say that some debt will happen in life, of course. My wife and I own a home and have a debt to the bank we are repaying on our home. When we lived in Puerto Rico, our cars died in the same week and we had to take out a car loan for one newer car. School loans are inevitable for many. However, it is possible to graduate from college with little, if any, school loans. I was able to finish my masters and doctorate degrees with no debt. I'm hardly that smart. So if I can do it then perhaps you can too!

GIVE IT AWAY

> Blessed are those who are generous. Proverbs 22:9

One of my favorite bands in college was The Red Hot Chili Peppers. They were awesome and I loved listening to them before going surfing. Their best song was "Give it Away." Several times a week, depending on how good the waves were and how far behind in school I was at the time, I would drive to Newport Beach with the Chili Peppers screaming this song through my Hyundai hatchback stereo: "Give it away, give it away, give it away now!"

Are you giving it away?

In college, I worked four days a week for four hours each day. My take-home pay was hardly something that would impress you, probably around a whopping eighty bucks a week. My excuse to not give then may be your excuse now: "Well, I don't make very much money and I have some debt I am paying down."

That may sound a bit harsh. When I was in college, a good friend explained the idea of giving to God even when we don't have much. He was right, and after studying the Bible and understanding God's command to give to his Church, I was convicted. As I began to give, I actually *enjoyed* it.

Yes, you read that correctly. I enjoyed it. It was an act of worship for me—it gave me joy to give to God's kingdom and obey him in this way. It will be an act of worship and produce joy for you too.

10-10-80

> Good planning and hard work lead to prosperity, but hasty shortcuts lead to poverty. Proverbs 21:5

When I was sixteen years old, my dad got me a job as a janitor at a local clothing store. I mopped, cleaned the windows, took out the trash, and became very skilled with a vacuum cleaner.

When I received my first paycheck, Dad said, "Shane, remember the 10-10-80 rule." I had no idea what he was talking about. All I could think of was cashing that check and spending it! My dad went on to explain that to apply this rule meant to give the first 10% to the church, to save the next 10%, and the remaining was meant to spend where it was needed. Well, according to my calculations (and my skills were hardly in math at this point in life) I needed all 100% to buy the surfboard I wanted.

Shoot. Really, Dad? Come on, way to spoil the fun!

The Bible is crystal clear when it comes to the wisdom of saving. Start now. This habit of saving will follow you and benefit you tremendously throughout your life.

Let me finish this chapter with an encouraging story of a student I recently interacted with at Arizona State University: "My second year here at ASU I learned of the opportunity to go on STINT, to go and live a year overseas sharing my faith with college students and other young people. This is when I realized I had a problem: my school loans. Graduating with approximately $39,000 in school debt was not very unusual, but I was very concerned about how I would begin paying back my loans right away. Fortunately, I was able to learn more about stewarding my finances as a student, and a few years later I was able to go on a one-year mission to East Asia."

QUESTIONS FOR REFLECTION AND DISCUSSION

God's Word speaks of money more than any other topic in the Bible. Why do you think God pays so much attention to our personal finances?

Read and discuss these verses concerning:
Debt: Proverbs 22:7; Romans 13:8; Romans 13:7; Psalm 73:21
Giving: Proverbs 22:9; Proverbs 17:17; 2 Corinthians 9:7; Malachi 3:10; Proverbs 3:9-10
Saving: Proverbs 21:10; Proverbs 21:5; Proverbs 6:6-8; Genesis 41:35-36; Proverbs 10:22; Proverbs 2:20; Ecclesiastes 5:10

In light of the Bible verses above, as you think of your own personal finances, what changes can you make to live out what you just read in Scripture?

CHAPTER 8

The Porn Problem

"Pornography on the Internet is the greatest challenge the church has faced in 2,000 years."
Josh McDowell

> How can a young person stay on the path of purity? By living according to your word. Psalm 119:9

JEFF FROM UCLA

After a somewhat awkward farewell, Jeff watched his parents drive toward the 405 freeway. The last few days had been a flurry of activity with orientations, campus tours, meeting a roommate who would be sharing his cramped quarters for the year, and several invitations from students to check out on-campus clubs. As a freshman at UCLA, far from home, no longer living under the roof or rules of his parents, Jeff looked forward to a year of experiencing new things.

The amount of campus clubs and organizations on his campus was overwhelming: fraternities, sororities, snowboard club, atheist club, philosophy club. There were dizzying amounts of opportunities to meet students and get involved. As he watched thousands of his peers filter through the main drag, Bruin Walk, Jeff felt a tap on his shoulder. Two students were behind him: "Excuse me, would you mind doing us a favor and filling out this spiritual interest survey?" The students from a Christian group on campus waited for an answer. Jeff grabbed the pencil they offered him, filled out a brief card and handed it back to them. He figured that was the end of that.

He was wrong.

Just a few hours later, Jeff was in his dorm room playing video games when there was a knock on his door. The same two students he met earlier, both juniors on campus, asked if they could come in and talk for a few minutes. Jeff had indicated on their survey that he had a slight interest in spiritual things and talking with someone about what it means to have a personal relationship with God. Just an hour later, Jeff's life changed forever when he, with the help of his new friends, made a decision to follow Jesus Christ.

He attended a Bible study in a dorm room where he learned more about God's love and purpose for his life. As a result of his understanding of God's love and forgiveness, Jeff wanted to share his faith and make an impact. After a study on God's heart for every people group, Jeff sensed God calling him to be a missionary overseas, specifically to other college students. He traveled on a two-week trip to East Asia to explore this new passion. These were some of the best two weeks of his life as he ministered to students in a country with very limited religious freedom. Jeff and his team visited five campuses in a region of five million people. Each campus had a group of students who were excited to interact and grow on a spiritual level with these American students. Jeff spent his two weeks discipling and sharing his faith with these students. When he left, he hoped that he would return.

Later, Jeff filled out his application for an evangelistic short-term mission trip. He was excited and passionate, as are many young people, to cross cultures and reach out to his peers. Unfortunately, Jeff was not accepted to participate on an international summer mission. He had a dream to cross cultures and share how Jesus has changed his life. However, this once-clear vision never became a reality. What happened?

Jeff was unable to go as a result of his addiction to pornography.

Pornography can serve as an escape for students in the midst of a chaotic campus life: "Students often use pornography to relieve boredom, anxiety, or depression in a way similar to their use of drugs or alcohol." [59] Many times I have seen eager students disqualified for overseas service because of their addiction to

Internet pornography—it's brutal and so sad.

The numbers are mind-blowing when it comes to this issue. Every thirty-nine minutes, a new pornographic video is produced. Every second, 372 Internet users are typing adult pornographic content into a search engine. According to apologist and author Josh McDowell, one out of every eight searches on the Internet is for erotic content; 80% of fifteen to seventeen-year-olds have been exposed to hardcore porn; and 56% of divorces are caused by porn. More than 70% of men between the ages of eighteen and thirty-four visit Internet porn sites each month.

Pornography is readily available to anyone, anywhere. Consider these statistics:

> It is certainly not news to most observers that the volume and popularity of sexually explicit materials on the Internet has increased exponentially over the past few years. Consider that between 1998 and 2007 it is estimated that the number of pornographic sites increased from 28,000 to 4.2 million and now account for 12 percent of all websites. Moreover, the subject of pornography reportedly comprises 25 percent of all search engine requests, and it is estimated that about 40 million adults regularly visit pornographic sites. [60]

This addiction typically hits more men than women and is more prevalent with college students. One particular study "conducted research with 18 male Christian college students who were struggling with Internet pornography addiction. All of these students indicated that the Internet helped them watch pornography because of its availability and easy access." [61] In general, studies show that pornography has a detrimental effect on values for college students and increases risky behavior. "As the pioneer study indicated, at this point it can be said that pornography may, in fact, be related to excessive participation in risky behaviors and may impact the way students view family formation values." [62]

Dr. Steve Shadrach is the founder and director of Student Mobilization. Dr. Shadrach agrees that pornography addiction is a significant "pitfall" for college students:

> It's especially hard for guys to bring "every thought captive to the obedience of Christ," because we are so stimulated by what we see. Most collegians have computers, and almost 100 percent have Internet access piped right into the students' rooms. In one survey, 95 percent of professed Christian college students agreed that looking at internet pornography is sinful, can hurt relationships, and can be addictive. Still 41 percent of the women and 68 percent of the men admitted intentionally viewing sexually explicit sites.[63]

Tens of millions of Americans are addicted to internet pornography. Consider these staggering statistics of pornography in our culture: [64]

1. 40 million Americans regularly visit pornographic web sites.
2. 2.5 billion emails sent each day contain the word porn.
3. 3. Sex is the number one topic searched on the Internet.
4. 70% of 18- to 24-year-old men in America visit pornographic sites in a typical month. 66% of men in their 20s and 30s also report being regular consumers of pornography.
5. According to pastors, the eight top sexual issues damaging to their congregation are: 57% pornography addiction; 34% sexually active never-married adults; 30% adultery of married adults; 28% sexually active teenagers; 16% sexual dissatisfaction; 14% unwed pregnancy; 13% sexually active previously married adults; and 9% sexual abuse.

WHEN PORN DISQUALIFIES

Matthew was a graduating senior at the University of Southern California. Matthew and twenty others from around California had gone on an international summer mission the previous summer to Melbourne, Australia. There are over 10,000 Chinese students studying abroad there; reaching these Chinese students while they are studying abroad is a strategic way to take the gospel to China. Matthew and his team saw several Chinese students become Christians as a result of their summer, and helped them grow in their new faith. He, along with several other of his friends from USC, then applied for a one-year STINT to go back to Melbourne and work with these Chinese students.

Like other college students, Matthew desired to share his life with others about how God had changed him. As a student, he was able to share his story of Jesus in his life with several of his friends who became followers of Jesus as well. Matthew hoped to return overseas and share more of his story. This idea of story-sharing and evangelism resonates with students like Matthew: "Evangelism is not convincing other people to accept the propositions you believe. Evangelism is inviting other people to begin a relationship with Jesus—to go on a journey with him and make his story their story." [65]

Matthew and his friends met weekly to pray for the Chinese students in Melbourne whom they hoped to minister to the following year. Matthew received an email from Cru explaining that he had not been accepted to go on STINT as a result of his addiction to pornography. [66] Several times a week, Matthew visited pornographic websites and had been doing so since he was in middle school. He was devastated and wondered if he would have a chance to go back to Australia.

Unfortunately, Matthew's story is all too common for students. In Matthew's case, he was asked to stay and intern with Cru in California. Matthew, with help from Cru, created a personal plan of development that addressed his addictions, and he was sent as a missionary overseas one year later.

The fact that Matthew was able to deal with his addiction to pornography is key and something I want all students to remember. Pornography may temporarily stop us from serving, *but only for a time*. Our God is a God of healing and forgiveness. He is a God who meets us in our struggles and makes us new.

TAKE NECESSARY STEPS

In light of this truth, allow me to share a few thoughts and necessary steps if you are struggling in this area. You can discuss this at the end of this chapter if you are reading this with a group.

TURN AROUND AND RECEIVE FORGIVENESS

> But if we confess our sins to him, he is faithful and just to forgive us our sins and to cleanse us from all wickedness. 1 John 1:9

When I was in elementary school, I remember finding a stack of pornographic magazines behind my backyard. Like any other "smart" kid, I took my newfound stash home and hid it at the back corner of my closet.

I was walking home from school the next day when my father pulled up to me in our fake-wood-paneled station wagon. In no uncertain terms, Dad told me to get in the car. I knew something wasn't right, and I knew exactly why he was picking me up. Dad went on to explain that he had found my hiding place. He was going camping and needed a sleeping bag; after searching the house, he eventually looked in the back corner of my closet.

I believe my dad going camping—and looking everywhere for a sleeping bag—was one of the better things that ever happened to me. As a result of that experience and my dad's wisdom, I learned how destructive porn is to our minds and how degrading it is to women. I also learned that though I may sin, no matter what I have done, I will always be forgiven. If I ask God, he will forgive me and help me turn from my sin.

TELL OTHERS

> Confess your sins to each other and pray for each other so that you may be healed. The earnest prayer of a righteous person has great power and produces wonderful results. James 5:16

A relationship with God is so much about experiencing community with others who share in this relationship. The Bible is very clear that one way we grow and deal with our sin is through others. Sharing your weaknesses and sin with others may not feel natural, but it is a main way God will grow us to become more like him.

I remember in college reading about how one of the ways God heals us and helps us to grow is through our friendships. At a Bible study, my leader read the above verse from James and shared some of his own struggles. He was very vulnerable and transparent with our small group, and we then spent some time praying for him. This was a great example to me of a leader who shared his struggles with a community and how a community helped in growth and healing.

BUILD YOUR HOUSE

> But the Holy Spirit produces this kind of fruit in our lives: love, joy, peace, patience, kindness, goodness, faithfulness, gentleness, and self-control. Galatians 5:22-23

I was in a surfing competition recently on the west side of Puerto Rico. As I prepared for my heat by stretching and studying the waves, a guy named Angelo came and sat down next to me. Angelo is a professional surfing coach (yes, there is such a thing!) and a judge for various surfing contests throughout the Caribbean and Central America. So when he asked if he could share some advice with me before I paddled out for my heat, my ear tuned in. He told me several times to "build my house."

"Shane, you need to paddle deep and to the inside of your competitors. As you do so, begin to build your house those first ten or so minutes of your heat."

Building your house in competition simply means to get busy early on in your heat and to make good and quick decisions that will help you later in the heat. After you make some good decisions on a few waves at the beginning of the heat, you have more confidence as bigger and better waves come. You get better as you build your house.

This metaphor of building our house works when it comes to overcoming our sin.

After you confess your sin, claim God's forgiveness, and share with others, you then move to building your house by practicing things that will help you later on in your day, in your week, and in your life. Each moment and each day, do things that will encourage growth in your life. Memorize scripture, join a Bible study or an accountability group, read your Bible, help others in your local church or movement on campus, and share your faith with your non-Christian friends.

As you take steps of faith in these areas, God will grow you to become more and more like him, and you will become a more fruitful follower of Jesus. Making these decisions, building your house—moment by moment, day by day, week by week, and month by month—will help you grow a foundation to live a pure life in and for God.

Last year, Jesse, a freshman from Arizona State University, shared this with me: "When I was in fifth grade, my friend showed me a pornographic website one day after school. I went home and began to look at other pornographic websites. Ever since that day I have viewed pornography at least four or five times a week. Now that I'm away at school it's easier than ever to get access to porn."

I wasn't at all surprised to hear this from Jesse. I also was not surprised to hear that he wanted to grow to become more like Jesus. He wanted to break his addiction to viewing pornography. I was excited to share how he could grow to become like Jesus and how he could be forgiven in this habit that was hurting him so much. I told him that God wanted to help him.

God wants to help you, too. God's Word is powerful. His people are instruments in helping us overcome addictions and temptations. Grab a friend and read the following verses together.

QUESTIONS FOR INDIVIDUAL OR GROUP REFLECTION

Before you go any further, read Psalm 119:9-11; 2 Timothy 2:22; 1 Peter 5:1-9; and 1 John 1:9.

How do you feel after reading this chapter? What is God saying to you as you read the above scripture?

What are some ways you can "build your house?"

What is the next step you can take in growing in the area of purity?

Read the article, "How Long Have You Been Looking at Porn?" You can find this on `cru.org`. Sit down with a friend or with your small group Bible study and discuss this together.

CHAPTER 9

WHEN MOM AND DAD SAY NO

"They are helping me pay for college, they pay my cell phone bill, and even my car insurance. If they say no, do I have another choice?"
Jill, sophomore at Northern Arizona University

> Hear, my son, your father's instruction, and forsake not your mother's teaching. Proverbs 1:8

Michelle was raised in a Christian home. Her parents had taught her about God and his love for her throughout her life. As she watched her parents leave the campus of UC Santa Barbara and head to Highway 101, she walked to the library to begin her campus tour. She was approached by two girls while waiting in line. They invited her to a large group meeting that night. Just a few hours later, Michelle was gathered with several hundred other students singing, playing games, and interacting with one another and studying the Bible over fish tacos and Mountain Dew.

That evening, Michelle met a student named Jill, who was a year younger than she was. Jill shared the idea of going on STINT. This new friend had just returned from a year-long missions trip during which she saw God do amazing things as she shared her faith with university students in Tokyo. Lives were changed, spiritual movements were built, and indigenous leaders were raised up over the year Jill and her teammates spent in Japan.

Through this new friendship, Michelle was inspired and challenged to go overseas to share her faith with university students in Tokyo. One evening, she called and asked me to fill out her reference form. "Please, Shane, I want to fast-track my application. I am so excited to go!"

Later that semester, she filled out an application and was accepted to be a short-term missionary with Cru. Michelle was excited as she prepared to take a year off of school and go share the reality of Jesus Christ with students in a culturally Buddhist country who have little to no understanding of God's love for them. The need was great and she was excited to be a part of sharing God's love with students who were eager to listen.

Nine months later, Michelle's team left for Japan. Unfortunately, Michelle was not going with them.

Why not? Because her parents said no.

Another obstacle students face as they consider going to the mission field is the opposition from their families. This is a high hurdle for students and a greater obstacle than most people think. [67] How does a young person, when not supported by their parents, go to the mission field? Many times I have sat across from a teary-eyed student who senses God calling him or her overseas for a week, a month, or a year and is struggling because his or her parents strongly oppose it. This chapter is not meant as a rebuke against well-meaning parents (I myself am a parent to four awesome kids), but simply should be noted as a difficult problem for missions-minded students.

Most students desire the approval of their parents when they consider becoming a missionary. The vast majority of students in all of the narrative interviews I performed in my doctoral program cited family as a major obstacle. One student from Arizona State University explained her concern as it relates to her family: "My parents, even though they are Christians, don't really understand the need. Plus, leaving my family for a summer would be hard." This obstacle is consistent with other research. Missions mobilizer and International Director of the Traveling Team, Todd Ahrend, writes, "The most serious peril under this head is that presented by home ties. The winds of opposition from father and mother have changed the course of many a man who has weathered other gales of fierce opposition." [68]

Many students who go as missionaries overseas come from non-Christian backgrounds. They become followers of Jesus while in college and have little, if any, spiritual support from their families or friends back home. One student told me:

> I think for me it is my parents and the rest of my family; my parents are not believers, and they just would not understand why I would want to spread the gospel and leave to be a missionary for a summer or for a year. There is really no support from family or from friends at home. I feel alone; maybe I shouldn't feel this way, but trying to know how to explain being a missionary to them is just so hard to think about.

When asked of the biggest obstacle as one considers missions, another student said, "Who is going to take care of my family? Who is going to look after my mom? Who is going to drive my brother and sister to school? It's like if I'm not there, what's going to happen?"

One student in his second year at Arizona State University, who had gone to East Asia the previous summer, said, "For me and other friends that went to East Asia, we had to deal with parents who were completely negative about me going. That was really hard to get through because they are Christians too."

Author and Professor J. Herbert Kane of Trinity Evangelical Divinity School writes of the tension students feel from Christian parents as they consider missions: "The opposition that comes from Christian parents is more silent and more subtle but none the less damaging. Such parents are in favor of Christian missions and give generously to the cause; but they are less than happy when their own son or daughter decides on a missionary career." [69]

This is echoed by Dr. Paul Borthwick, author of dozens of books on student missions and professor at Gordon College. He stated in a conversation with me that "well-meaning parents is one of the biggest obstacles students face as they consider missions." Many parents will give to missions organizations, support missionaries, and even sit on their church missions committee. However, when their own children decide to consider missions, they can be unsupportive.

AN OLD ISSUE

The student mobilizer John Mott (who we looked at in a previous chapter) was held back from going to the mission field by his parents. The Student Volunteer Movement, initiated by Mott as a college student, eventually was responsible for sending almost 21,000 missionaries to the field. Mott was a visionary and was known as "that young man who thinks in continents." [70] He was passionate about missions and of reaching college students as he traveled across the Atlantic Ocean over one hundred times, averaging thirty-four days on the ocean for fifty years!

As Mott recruited students for foreign missions with the SVM, he addressed the issue of family, noting that even Christian leaders were against their own children going into the mission field: "Not long since the chairman of a denominational missionary society protested when his own daughter expressed her desire to become a volunteer." [71]

HONORING YOUR PARENTS

Just a few months ago, Kiva, a student from Cal State Fresno, called me. She was interested in missions. Kiva had been overseas for a summer mission and sensed God calling her to go back for one or two years as soon as she graduated. After listening to her passion and excitement to go, I asked her, "Awesome, so what's the problem? Why haven't you filled out an application?" Her answer was a common one: "Well, my parents are against it."

It's so important to honor our parents. God takes this very seriously and even commands this regardless of our age. But how do we honor our parents when we disagree? What if we want to do something that we know God desires, and our parents flat out forbid it?

This was essentially the question Kiva was asking me. She wanted to go overseas as a missionary for a year. Her parents wanted her to go to graduate school right away to become a teacher. She asked me, "Shane, what am I supposed to do?"

I shared three important elements in relating to our parents, especially when we disagree over something we believe is very important:

Have an Adult Conversation

A gentle answer turns away wrath, but a harsh word stirs up anger. Proverbs 15:1

Kiva explained that she had only mentioned her hopes and dreams over the phone to her parents. I then gave her an assignment: go home during your next available weekend and let your parents know beforehand that you want to talk with them about something that is very important to you. Sit down with your parents and first let them know that you desire to honor them with your life. You respect them and want to make them proud. Then tell them you have a dream and passion to go overseas for a year (or whatever it is you are discussing). Initiate with them. Look them in the eye. Thank them for their love and concern for you. This is an adult conversation.

Listen

Let the wise listen and add to their understanding. Proverbs 1:5

I can't even tell you how much better life would be if we listened. Just ask my wife—I'm hardly the best listener! After you share this with your parents, let them talk. Do not interrupt them. Even if you feel they are not being reasonable or you sense they are not understanding you.

Love

We love because he first loved us. 1 John 4:19

After the conversation, tell your parents that you love them. This will show honor and respect to them. Also, your simple acts of initiating and listening to them will help them feel loved and will grow you in your relationship with them.

My oldest daughter recently asked me if we could have a "private talk." I was actually a little nervous and couldn't imagine what she wanted to talk about! The next day Kirra and I sat down and she actually read a letter to me asking for more freedom with her life (staying up later, more time on her iPad, time with friends, etc.). She initiated time and conversation with me. She listened to me. She showed and told me that she loved me. My fifteen-year-old daughter had an adult conversation with me.

Through my tears, I thanked my daughter. I went to bed that night feeling honored by my teenager. I'll let you imagine how much she got of what she asked for, but let's just say she made out pretty well.

Over the past twenty-four years of ministry with young people, I have spoken with numerous concerned parents. As a parent myself, I understand their concerns. I also realize that the vast majority of concerns parents have are valid and can be addressed through consistent communication with their children. An excellent resource we use with students as they speak with their parents is called Just For Parents. This can be found at `www.cru.org`.

This resource helps parents with their concerns regarding the organization of Cru, finances, safety, leadership, communication, the logistics of the trip itself, and much more.

This is a great opportunity for you to honor your father and mother as you consider going overseas. Read through this together and ask them if they have any questions or concerns. Use this as an opportunity to grow in your relationship with your parents.

Let me conclude this chapter with this encouraging story from Alexis, a former student at the University of California Davis:

"This time last year, my friend challenged me to pray about going to Tokyo for a summer to share my faith and disciple Japanese students. It was a life-changing summer as I learned so much about Japanese culture; I was able to make friends with several Japanese students and share with them my own story of how God has impacted my life. I even was able to lead a person into a relationship with Jesus, and we are in touch all the time! I almost did not go to Japan after talking with my parents. At first they flat-out forbade me from going. They said they wanted me to go to summer school. After some hard but understanding conversations with my parents they gave me their blessing."

Alexis spent the summer overseas as a missionary sharing

the reality of Jesus Christ with other university students. God used her life to bring other students to him. God worked in and through her in Japan. But just as much, God used the conversations with her parents before she left to draw them closer in their relationship.

I hope that God will do the same for you.

QUESTIONS FOR REFLECTION OR DISCUSSION

Throughout history, students have felt tension from their families when considering missions. How do you think your parents would respond if you spoke with them about going overseas as a missionary?

Read these Bible verses: Exodus 20:12; Ephesians 6:1-3; Deuteronomy 5:16; Leviticus 19:3; Proverbs 1:8; Proverbs 10:1; Proverbs 30:17.

How do these verses hit you as you think about your relationship with your parents?

If you are considering going overseas as a short-term missionary, have you spoken to your parents yet? How did they respond?

CHAPTER 10

AVOIDING MEXICAN JAILS AND DISCERNING THE WILL OF GOD

"A coworker sees what needs to be done and simply does it. We become so close to God that we do not have to wait to hear his words. We don't have to be asked."
Dallas Willard

"The question God cares about most is not 'Where should I live' but 'Do I love the Lord with all my heart?'"
Kevin DeYoung, *Just Do Something*

"I wish God would just tell me what to do! How do I know?"
Student, University of Oklahoma

I was meeting with a student at UC Santa Barbara and was asked a question I had been asked many times before.

My friend Carlos had several opportunities for his summer. Should he take the local internship he was offered with a software company? What about moving home for the summer and spending time with his family? Or perhaps taking a few classes in the summer session? What about going on a summer mission? So many options!

A major stumbling block for young people as they consider missions is in the area of students' discernment of God's will. The common question asked of me as a minister and missionary is: How do I know God's will for my future? Young people (most people, to be honest) are confused and derailed as they "try to figure out" what God wants them to do in the area of missions and their lives in general. As one author writes, "There has been no bigger tragedy, no bigger misunderstanding, and no bigger enemy in missions than the confusion of the missionary call." [72]

My friend Claude Hickman, author and U.S. Director of the missionary organization The Traveling Team, challenges young people with the simple idea that God calls people into a shared life with him. There is not always a specific path God wants us to take. Hickman speaks of the importance of obeying God. God is not so much telling us what to do in every decision, but pointing us to abide. God gives us a compass, not a map, to live our lives. Hickman and other youth ministers agree: Understanding the will of God is a major barrier in students considering missions.

A SURF TRIP AND A MEXICAN JAIL

Life is constantly bringing us decisions. Some are big and some are small. My family and I made a big decision to move from our home in Southern California to Puerto Rico a few years ago for the purpose of working with college students for two years. I've had many friends ask me how I know whether or not that was the right decision.

Do you ever make a decision and then think, "Was that the right call?" "How do I know it's really what God wants?" Do you ever feel nervous about or second-guess your decisions? How do we rest in our decisions?

I rest in those decisions by reminding myself that God is always present, *always near*, even in my doubts and fears.

I remember a particular surf trip to Mexico with my best friend way back in college. The waves were so good on that trip, but what I remember most was being pulled over by the Mexican police. This was normal and actually happened often on our surf trips.

The way it would normally play out is we'd ask what the problem was, listen to the police bring up several false and ridiculous charges of speeding or littering, and then offer to pay them $30 cash. That number would normally double, and then we would be on our way across the border.

Not this time.

My friend Jim was in no mood to negotiate, even though he

had left shotgun shells in his truck from a previous hunting trip. The cops were not happy about those shells. But Jim said he would pay no fine, and next the cops said they would take us to the jail for processing.

I was getting nervous.

Jim looked at the cops and simply said, "Okay, let's do that. Good idea, guys. Let's go to the jail. In fact, I'm a friend of the police chief. We built houses together here in Rosarito last summer. Let's go see him and what he has to say."

Because Jim knew the police chief, we were allowed to get back in the truck and drive across the border. The police looked at me and said, "You can go, too; you're with him." I was with Jim so I had nothing to worry about.

All over the Bible we see a God who is always with us, always present in the big and small decisions. In the Old Testament, God calls Jeremiah to be a prophet to the nations, not just to the nation of Judah, *but to the nations*. A big job. How does Jeremiah respond? This soon-to-be great leader responds with fear, anxiety, and excuses. Their interaction goes like this:

God: *"Before I formed you in the womb I knew you, and before you were born I consecrated you; I appointed you a prophet to the nations."*

Jeremiah: *"Lord God, I do not know how to speak, for I am only a youth."*

God: *"I am with you."*

Jeremiah does obey God. And he was no doubt encouraged knowing that God would be with him as he followed the Lord's will. God was with him so he had nothing to worry about.

The God spoken of in Jeremiah is the same God we speak of—and hear from—today. No matter what decision you make as you live out God's will, remember God's never-ending presence in your life. Remember that as you think about the small and big decisions in life while you pursue the will of God.

As I've worked with students all over the world, I've noticed three ways they approach God's will: the conventional approach, the confusing approach, and the calling approach. Let me briefly explain those below.

THE CONVENTIONAL APPROACH: GIVE ME A DETAILED BLUEPRINT!

Many of us are infatuated with the idea that we must have a very detailed and specific call from God to go into missions. God can, at times, speak to us very specifically when he calls us to do something, as we see with Jeremiah in the example above. In my experience, however, this does not always happen. When we wait for God to tell us exactly what to do, we create a problem.

My previous pastor from when we lived in Southern California, Larry Osborne, writes of the problem this way: "The problem stems from a concept many of us have been taught from birth. We've been led to believe that God has a highly detailed blueprint for our life that includes a specific, preordained job, career, house, spouse, car—and everything in between." [73]

Pastor Larry continues to explain that searching for God's will is hardly simple for most:

> There's no cosmic Easter egg hunt required to see who can find God's will and who gets left with an empty basket. But unfortunately, that's how many of us feel. The problem stems from a concept many of us have been taught from birth. We've been led to believe that God has a highly detailed blueprint for our life that includes a specific, preordained job, career, house, spouse, car—and everything in between. As a result, we spend a lot of time looking for that special person, place, or thing that we think God has set aside just for us. It's the egg we hunt for. [74]

A blueprint is very specific, very detailed, and must be followed precisely or the overall plan will be at risk. My brother-in-law is an architect and my father is a developer. My brother-in-law draws up highly detailed plans then passes the blueprint on to my father and the builder. My father, the builder, follows the details of the blueprint. If my father fails to follow even a small detail of the blueprint, the whole project can fall apart.

Unfortunately, this is how many young people approach discernment of God's will, even as they consider a short-term opportunity to be a missionary. They want a detailed blueprint. You don't always need a detailed blueprint!

Why should we avoid this conventional approach to God's will? First, the implication that God's will is a detailed blueprint for one to follow implies that a single wrong turn can make everything collapse. Friends, please understand that God is indeed concerned with what we do. But God is much more concerned with who we are than about dictating our lives according to a blueprint.

God has a plan for you—not a blueprint. His plan is that you walk with him and become like his son Jesus as you live day to day. I think young people, all people, feel freedom when they hear this. As Micah 6:8 states, "He has shown you, O mortal, what is good. And what does the Lord require of you? To act justly and to love mercy and to walk humbly with your God." Or as St. Augustine said: "Love God and do what you desire." In other words, it is the quality of one's heart and intention that is most important to God. *He is most concerned with who we are.*

God will likely call you to go to certain places, to do certain things for him, to take a certain role or position. We see God call people to specific things throughout the Bible. However, God first and foremost calls us to follow and be like him. As the apostle Paul writes in Romans 12:2: "Do not conform any longer to the pattern of this world, but be transformed by the renewing of your mind. Then you will be able to test and approve what God's will is—his good, pleasing, and perfect will." God's will is not about a detailed blueprint; it is about renewing our minds.

God's will is concerned with God's wishes. And God wishes us to be like the person of Jesus, renewing our minds and growing in his likeness.

THE CONFUSING APPROACH: JUST SHOW ME WHAT YOU WANT!

The conventional approach to knowing God's will is just one approach we gravitate to. We can also follow a much more mysterious approach, what I refer to as "the confusing approach" to knowing the will of God. I recently heard a student say, "I just wish God would show me what he wants!" It was spoken as if God's desires were hidden. Yet God's will is not a mystery to unravel; there is nothing hidden about God's will for you. As pastor Kevin DeYoung writes, "God's will is not an unexplained labyrinth whose center we are supposed to discover." [75]

God's will has to do with the things we already know. We don't always know how things will turn out. However, we do know several things outlined in scripture that are God's will.

1. God wills that we have a relationship with him.
Paul wrote to a young pastor named Timothy, "God desires all people to be saved and to come to the knowledge of the truth" (2 Timothy 2:4). 2 Peter 3:9 speaks of God's will that everyone knows him: "The Lord is not slow to fulfill his promise as some count slowness, but is patient toward you, not wishing that any should perish, but that all should reach repentance." Jesus speaks of God's love for every person when he says in John 3:16: "For God so loved the world, that he gave his only Son, that whoever believes in him should not perish but have eternal life." God's will is first that you enter into a personal relationship with him. This is what God created you for.

2. God's will is that we be filled and controlled with the Holy Spirit.
The Bible speaks often of God's desire for us to be filled, to be empowered, by his Holy Spirit: "Therefore do not be foolish, but understand what the will of the Lord is. And do not get drunk with wine, for that is debauchery, but be filled with the Spirit" (Romans 8:14). To the church in Galatia, the apostle Paul writes, "But if you are led by the Spirit, you are not under the law" (Galatians 5:18). Scripture is clear that if we want wisdom to know God's will, we must be Spirit-filled. As we are filled with and directed by the Holy Spirit, we will know what God desires for us. Something to remember is that as a Christian who believes in Christ, you are guided by the Holy Spirit, and you can trust your decisions. And as we grow closer to God through his word and Spirit, we will know God's will!

Something I find interesting is that the Old Testament speaks much more specifically to people about what God actually wants them to do. God tells Moses to lead the Israelites. God tells Jeremiah to lead his nation. God tells Jonah to warn Nineveh. He speaks to his people clearly about what he wants them to do. In the New Testament, instead of telling his followers more of what he wants them to do, he tells them more of who he wants them to follow and become. This happens after God has sent his Holy Spirit to live inside of his followers in the book of Acts. As I've come to understand this, I am more compelled to walk with God and be empowered by him.

3. God's will is that we be set apart to be used by him.

All over God's word, we read about his desire for us to become more and more like him. 1 Thessalonians 4:3 says, "For this is the will of God, your sanctification." Hebrews 10:10 says, "By this will we have been sanctified through the offering of the body of Jesus Christ once for all." To be sanctified means to be set apart, to be made holy for God's use. This fancy word simply means to become more like Jesus. Our role as we live our lives is not so much to find something, but to become someone more like the person of Jesus.

In the Old Testament, we see God using special tools in the temple to bring him glory. The Bible says these tools are set apart to be used in a way that will bring God honor and praise. Then in the New Testament, God uses the same word to describe his people, to describe us! We too are set apart to be used to bring God honor and praise.

Do you believe this? Ask yourself that question right now: "Do I believe that God has set me apart to walk with him and influence others?" Believe it, friends. God has set you apart to influence others, and to help others experience a relationship with him.

4. God's will is that we do what we want.

This sounds almost unspiritual, doesn't it? Yet this has a strong theological foundation. Live a life obedient to God and go from there. Walk with Jesus and see where God leads you. Abide and seek him in life and he will direct you.

See what God says about this in Philippians 2:12-13: "Therefore, my beloved, as you have always obeyed, so now, not only as in my presence but much more in my absence, work out your own salvation with fear and trembling, for it is God who works in you, both to his will and to work for his good pleasure." As God works in our lives, and as we submit to the guidance of the Holy Spirit and to the process of sanctification, God motivates and guides us to make decisions that are in line with God's will. As one author writes: "the biblical doctrine of providence suggests that God works within the redeemed believer to form desires which accord with his will." [76]

In other words, God will make his desires your desires as you grow in your relationship with him.

I want to help young people understand that as they practice right intentions and grow in Christlikeness, they can trust God to guide them throughout their lives.

It's important to state the obvious here. The four steps above are not meant to model a program that, if properly followed, will result in knowing every aspect of God's will. The will of God in the life of a Christian is to be the result of a growing relationship. The steps above merely point to the aspects of that relationship.

THE CALLING APPROACH: "I'M WAITING FOR GOD TO TELL ME"

"No aspect of Christian mission is more puzzling than this problem of a call." [77]

In my conversations with students about missions, the most common concern or excuse is, "But I'm not sure if God has called me." It's as if one needs an extra special revelation to be called as a missionary, and a less special revelation to be called to another job. I refer to this as the "calling" approach to finding the will of God.

I would argue that calling, or being called by God to do something, should be applied even more so when considering not going into missions. As one missionary suggests, "There is a general obligation resting upon Christians to see that the Gospel of Jesus Christ is preached to the world. You and I need no special call to apply that general call of God to our lives." [78] A general calling is already there. This also addresses what some call the "Lightning Bolt Calling Myth." This myth suggests that most young people think they must have a miraculous calling experience in order to cross cultures to spread the good news of Jesus. You don't need a special calling from God to share your faith in Jesus with anyone in any place.

God is calling all of us to live a life that is pleasing to him. It really is that simple. Walk with God and make decisions as they come. As you walk with him, and become more like Jesus, and do what he wants, God will use you in ways that will expand his kingdom and change the lives of people you come into contact with. God especially does this with young people!

One of my favorite stories of young people and global missions is about a young, nineteen-year-old student named Bruce Olsen. He had questions about God's will but he didn't allow them to take away from his heart's desire to share the reality of Jesus Christ. As Olsen grew in his understanding of God's love for him when he was a student, he sensed God calling him to South America to share knowledge of Jesus Christ with the Montilone Indians.

After being rejected by several missionary agencies, Olson left Penn State University and, despite his father's forbidding, moved to Colombia. Going against the wishes of his family was not easy for him. The impact Olson had is historic. Twenty years later, Olson had translated the Montilone language, founded eight bilingual schools, opened ten health centers, gave seven college scholarships to Montilone Indians, translated the New Testament, and literally changed the physical and spiritual world of the Montilone tribe. All of this came from a nineteen-year-old college student who sensed God calling him to be Christ-like and share Jesus with everyone around him.

Bruce Olson, as a young college dropout, made a historic impact in worldwide missions.

You can too.

QUESTIONS FOR INDIVIDUAL AND GROUP REFLECTION

Look again at the three ways many people view calling. How have you typically viewed calling? The conventional, the confusing, or the calling approach?

Have you ever thought that God's will is that we do what we want? Explain this in your own words.

How would you respond to someone if they asked you right now, "How do I determine God's will for my life?"

CHAPTER 11

WRAPPING UP: GO MEANS DON'T STAY

"Salvation has come to us because it's on its way to someone else."
Todd Ahrend, *In This Generation*

> "Go and make disciples of all nations."
> Jesus Christ, Matthew 28:19

I was sitting in Moby Gym at Colorado State University for our biennial national staff conference. I was towards the back as I had barely arrived in time for the message. (I had to finish up a very important volleyball game.) I may have been surrounded by six thousand other missionaries, but it felt like Dr. Tony Evans was speaking directly to me. This was no doubt the best sermon I had ever heard. Dr. Evans was preaching about Jesus's words in Matthew 28: "Go therefore and make disciples of all nations."

What does Jesus mean when he tells his followers to *go*? What exactly does go mean? This Great Commission text is written five times in the New Testament (Matthew 28:18-20, Mark 16:15, Luke 24:46-48, John 20:21, and Acts 1:8). Jesus strongly emphasizes his command to go and share the love of God with the world.

Friends, don't overthink it. As Dr. Evans preached to me that day: "Go means don't stay."

WHY SHORT-TERM MISSIONS MATTER

"I'm not sure I'm ready for this. I'm not sure if I believe yet, but I want to learn more." My new friend Javier and I had just spent an hour talking about God and Jesus, friends, values, and the future.

I had met him through a survey he filled out when a short-term missions team had visited Puerto Rico. It was a great conversation and we became friends. I pray for him on a regular basis and I hope to see him begin a relationship with God soon.

As I drove home that day I thought of the privilege I have in doing what I do. It's such a privilege to share with students about how they can have a personal relationship with the living God. My friend Javier had never heard what I had shared with him.

Think about that. He had never heard.

As I mentioned above, I met him because of a short-term team that had visited us just a few weeks prior. I loved it when short-term missions teams visited us when we lived overseas; they really helped us reach students on campus and grow what God was already doing.

Let me be the first to invite you on a short-term mission. Go somewhere for a week, for a month, or for a year. I don't really care where you go. Just go somewhere.

God's plan is that we live a long-term missional life. Short-term missions (a week, six weeks, one or two years) in many ways helps us live long-term for God as we introduce others to Jesus. As one who has hosted these short-term teams, allow me to share three very simple reasons why short-term missions matter.

1. They Matter Because Long-Term Missionaries Need Your Help

A few months ago I read a blog post in which the writer was going on and on about how short-term missions are overrated. They are a hassle for those living on location and receiving the team. They create more work. The blog said sometimes they're just not worth it.

Wrong. I totally disagree.

As a result of short-term teams visiting us, we saw people come to know Jesus, we saw students who were on the fringe of our group become more involved, and we were encouraged as a team.

I met with a pastor in Puerto Rico who wanted to hear more about how we could partner together. He said we were on the front lines of what he wanted his church to be doing. It was an awesome conversation about partnering together to help people see how Jesus is working around them. I asked him how he came to know so much about who we are as a group and what God had called us to do on campus. He had met with the leader of our short-term team from the past summer. This team was in and out of there in one month. But I feel like that short trip moved us forward about a year.

The leader of that team, my good buddy, Joe Priola, explained to my pastor that in some ways our group is like an ambulance service. We want to pick up students and drive them to Jesus. We are an ambulance service for my pastor's church, and for other churches.

2. They Matter Because They Are Biblical

I am not at all saying that short-term missions is the end-all; of course not. The longer we have missionaries on the field, the better opportunity there is to raise up national leaders. It's all about nationally-led spiritual movements. Once we see nationals lead, we stay and serve under them, we or go somewhere else.

But God has a history of using short-term missions. How long do you think the apostle Paul spent planting those churches we are always reading about in the New Testament? Did he stay in those places for five years or more at a time?

Nope. He was in those cities briefly—read more about Paul's STINT year in Antioch in Acts 11 and his ninety-day short-term mission in Ephesus in Acts 19—and then coached and encouraged the leaders from a distance. Sometimes he even coached and mentored these churches from a prison cell.

3. They Matter Because They Bless Both Sides of The Ocean

I spent ten years as a campus minister at UC Santa Barbara. One student I worked with for several years was my friend John. John invested a summer while he was at UCSB and went to Tokyo on a summer mission. John came back from that summer on fire. He went on to start a group on campus called Epic. Epic is a contextualized ministry that focuses on helping Asian-American students know and grow in Jesus.

As the director of the campus, I was thrilled. I had this student come back from a summer and ask me if I could help him reach out to students. Where did he get this vision? Was it from me mentoring him? Was it from our Bible study? Nope. (But I would like to think so!) God clearly gave John a vision to reach Asian American students as a result of spending a summer on mission in Tokyo. His summer blessed not just those students in Japan but those at UCSB as well. The group John started seventeen years ago at UCSB continues today.

We recently had a fall retreat in Puerto Rico—"Retiro de Otoño." During the last meeting, I looked around the audience and counted twenty-six students representing six universities. I thought of the other twenty or so students who weren't at the retreat but were still involved with us. I was encouraged as I thought of how many students were involved when we arrived the previous year—zero.

We met many of those students as a result of short-term mission teams who came in to help us. They were such a blessing. If and when you go on a short-term mission, I am sure you will be a blessing as well.

It really is amazing how Christianity has spread these last two thousand years. As you have read in this book, God has always—always—used young people who step out in faith to spread the great news of Jesus. The last few hundred years is especially remarkable. "World Christianity is the result of the great missionary expansion of the last two centuries. That expansion, whatever one's attitude to Christianity may be, is one of the most remarkable facts of human history," suggests historian Ruth Tucker. [79] A remarkable fact of the expansion of Christianity is the youth God has empowered in growing worldwide Christianity. Students have played a significant part in global evangelization.

The past informs us that God has had a very significant and strategic role for young people in advancing the good news of Jesus Christ. There's no reason to believe God will use students any differently in the future as he brings people into a relationship with him. Throughout history, God has clearly called young people to cross cultures to help others experience a relationship with him.

Now is no different.

I love this story of a young person who recently returned from a short-term mission in Central America:

> The second day on campus in our city here in El Salvador we walked up to several random students and asked them about life as a university student. We wanted to learn more so we asked them a lot of questions. One student we spoke with that first day is Olivia. The past seven weeks have been an amazing journey as we have gotten to know her more and more. We have had the pleasure of hanging out with Olivia in a variety of circumstances: from when the brakes went out on our car while driving to get pizza, to having intentional Bible studies—it's been fun to live life with her. One of the first times we hung out we shared the vision of Vida Estudiantil (Cru in Latin America) with her and our desire to give every student on every campus an opportunity to hear the Gospel. Olivia replied, with tears in her eyes, that she had been praying for someone to help her be a light on her college campus.

There are millions of young college students around the world who are just like Olivia. They need help in understanding how they can grow in a personal relationship with God. They know God is there. They know they need forgiveness. They want to walk with God now and for the rest of their lives. They need someone to tell them.

I think it should be you.

One day back when I was a college student (a long, long time ago), I was at work and able to talk with my friend Arturo, from southern Mexico, about how he could experience a relationship with God through Jesus Christ. I worked in the kitchen with Arturo and we were usually the last ones to finish the shift.

After work, we would always sit down on the back dock and talk. Arturo spoke very little English, and I spoke very little Spanish, and in some ways we helped each other learn the other's language that year. After a month or so, I really wanted to talk to Arturo about how God was real, how God had changed my life, and how Arturo could know God, too. I was able to read a presentation of the gospel in Spanish to Arturo and he became a Christian.

This interaction with Arturo and our friendship had an impact on me in so many ways. I realized I wanted to see how I could be a missionary for a summer or for a year or two and share my faith cross-culturally. As I became more interested, I also came to understand my own inadequacies and shortcomings. There were so many obstacles that seemed to be in the way of my sharing God's love as a short-term missionary. Specifically, a few of the bigger obstacles for me were in the area of finances and understanding God's will. As God began to help me understand how to deal with these barriers, I was able to go on a short-term mission in college.

God has big plans for you. He desires to send students to share his love with people around the world. My prayer is that this book has motivated you to consider going with your friends and giving a summer or a year to global evangelization. I pray that you have come to a better understanding how God can use you to reach people all over the world.

The prophet Isaiah wrote down the words of God: "I will also make you a light of the nations so that my salvation may reach to the end of the earth." You have been made by the living God to be a light that will reach to the end of the earth. Join your peers throughout history who have been world changers through the power of Jesus Christ. Your world, and many others, will never be the same.

QUESTIONS FOR INDIVIDUAL OR GROUP REFLECTION

What is your biggest takeaway from this book?

As you consider God's plan for reaching the nations, what part do you think he has for you to play?

How can your life lead others to understanding God's love for them?

NOTES

1. In Campus Crusade for Christ (Cru) parlance, a "STINT" is a "Short Term International" mission that lasts for one or two years.

2. Walvoord and Zuck, *The Bible Knowledge Commentary* (Colorado Springs: 1985), 1148.

3. For more on David's life and leadership as it relates to missions, see Todd Ahrend's book, *The Abrahamic Revolution: God's Mission in Motion* (Colorado Springs: Dawson Media, 2011).

4. Regina Diane Sullivan, "Woman With a Mission: Remembering Lottie Moon and the Women's Missionary Union" (PhD diss., University of North Carolina at Chapel Hill, 2002), xii.

5. Catherine B. Allen, "The Legacy of Lottie Moon," *International Bulletin of Missionary Research* 17, no. 4 (October 1993): 146.

6. Ibid.

7. Mark Letter, *Josiah's Reform and Jeremiah's Scroll: Historical Calamity and Prophetic Response* (Sheffield, TN: Sheffield Phoenix Press, 2006), 58.

8. Dan Hayes, *Fireseeds of Spiritual Awakening* (Orlando: Cru Press, 2007), 24.

9. For another resource on Ruth and Esther, see Warren W. Wiersbe, *Be Committed: Doing God's Will Whatever the Cost*

(Colorado Springs, CO: David C. Cook Publishers, 1995).

10. Drora Oren, "Esther: The Queen of Jewish Persia," *NASHIM: A Journal of Jewish Women's Studies and Gender Issues* (2009): 139.

11. Todd Ahrend, *The Abrahamic Revolution: God's Mission in Motion* (Colorado Springs: Dawson Media, 2010), 92.

12. `http://www.wycliffe.org/About.aspx` (accessed March 2, 2012).

13. Leonard Sweet and Frank Viola, *Jesus: A Theography* (Nashville: Thomas Nelson, 2012) 137.

14. Ibid., 140.

15. Scott McNight, "The Mary We Never Knew: Why the Mother of Jesus Was More of a Revolutionary Than We've Been Led to Believe," *Christianity Today* (December 2006): 30.

16. Ibid., 63.

17. Scott McNight, "The Mary We Never Knew: Why the Mother of Jesus Was More of a Revolutionary Than We've Been Led to Believe," *Christianity Today* (December 2006): 30.

18. Thomas C. Oden, *The African Memory of Mark: Reassessing Early Church Tradition* (Downers Grove: InterVarsity Press, 2011), 22.

19. Oden, *The African Memory of Mark*, 138.

20. Walvoord and Zuck, 181.

21. Timothy A. Betty, "The Work of an Evangelist As Understood by Paul's Disciple Timothy" (Master's thesis, Western Conservative Baptist Seminary, 1993), 22.

22. David M. Howard, *Student Power in World Missions* (Downers Grove, IL: InterVarsity Press, 1979), 62.

23. See George G. Hunter, *The Celtic Way of Evangelism: How Christianity Can Reach the West...Again* (Nashville: Abingdon Press, 2000).

24. Much is written about why the Church did not expand as rapidly before the year 1700. For a thorough description, see: J. Herbert Kane, *A Concise History of Christian of Christian World Missions* (Grand Rapids: Baker Book House, 1978).

25. George G. Hunter, *The Celtic Way of Evangelism: How Christianity Can Reach the West...Again* (Nashville: Abingdon Press, 2000).

26. George Hunter, 35.

27. Ruth A. Tucker, *From Jerusalem to Irina Jaya: A Biographical History of Christians Missions* (Grand Rapids: Zondervan, 2004), 100.

28. Gary S. Kinkel, *Christian Life and Witness: Count Zinzendorf's 1738 Berlin Speeches* (Eugene: Pickwick Publications, 2010), xv.

29. Phil Anderson, *The Lord of the Ring: Uncovering the Secret Origins of Praying* 24-7 (Ventura: Regal Books, 2007), 38.

30. Leonard Sweet, *The Greatest Story Never Told: Revive Us Again* (Nashville: Abingdon Press, 2012), 7.

31. Alice Rouse, ed. *The Essential Works of John Wesley: Selected Sermons, Essays, and Other Writings* (Uhrichsville: Barbour Publishing, 2011), Adobe Digital Edition eBook.

32. Much has been written on young people who have led in world missions. There are many names I am unable to dig into such as William Carey.

33. David M. Howard, *Student Power in World Missions* (Illinois: InterVarsity Press, 1979), 74.

34. Ibid.

35. Tucker, 131.

36. Ibid., 132.

37. David M. Howard, *Student Power in World Missions* (Illinois: InterVarsity Press: 1979), 68.

38. Howard, 70.

39. Robert P. Wilder, *The Student Volunteer Movement: Its Origin and Early History* (New York: The Student Volunteer Movement, 1935), 9.

40. Jessica Ahrend, "Grace Wilder" http://www.thetravelingteam.org/gracewilder (accessed September 23, 2013).

41. Todd Ahrend, *In This Generation: Looking to the Past to Reach the Present* (Colorado Springs, CO: Dawson Media, 2010), 59.

42. Todd Ahrend, *In This Generation: Looking to the Past to Reach the Present* (Colorado Springs: Dawson Press: 2010), 60.

43. Steve Shadrach, *The Fuel and the Flame: 10 Keys to Ignite Your College for Jesus Christ* (Waynesboro: 2003), 19.

44. Robert P. Wilder, *The Student Volunteer Movement: Its Origins and Early History* (New York: The Student Volunteer Movement, 1935), 9.

45. Ibid., 12-13.

46. This conference is known as the Mount Hermon Project where a group of one hundred students signed a declaration stating they would enter into foreign missionary service.

47. Tucker, 239.

48. Jesse R. Wilson, "Some 1921 Missionaries and the SVM" in Student Volunteer Movement Bulletin (New York: The Student for Volunteer Movement for Foreign Missions), 17-18.

49. Roger D. Woods, "A World of Thought of John Mott" (PhD. diss., University of Iowa, 1965).

50. Michael Parker, *The Kingdom Of Character: The Student Volunteer Movement for Foreign Missions* (Lanham, MD: University Press of America, 1998), 1.

51. Fennel P. Turner, ed. *Students and the World-Wide Expansion of Christianity: Address Delivered Before the Seventh International Convention of the Student Volunteer Movement for Foreign Missions* (New York: Forgotten Books, 2012), 17.

52. Luther Deloraine Wishard, *The Students' Challenge to the Churche: A Plea for a Forward Movement in World Evangelization* (Chicago: Fleming H. Revell Company, 1899), 23.

53. William M. Beam, "Factors in the Development of the Student Volunteer Movement for Foreign Missions" (PhD diss., University of Chicago, 1943), 3.

54. This was observed at the University of Puerto Rico in Aguadilla, InterAmericana University in Aguadilla, University of Puerto Rico in Mayaguez, and InterAmericana University in San German, Puerto Rico in September of 2013.

55. Josh Cooper, *Hold Fast: The Mission of God and the Obstacles of Man* (Colorado Springs: Book Villages, 2013), 105-106.

56. American Student Assistance. `http://www.asa.org/policy/resources/stats` (accessed July 4, 2013).

57. Lillian Guerra, "Graduating a Debtor Nation: Shameless Confessions of a Dissenting Citizen," *The History Teacher* 41 no. 2 (February 2008): 208.

58. Ibid. 106.

59. Jerry D. Hudson, "The Experience of Male Undergraduate Christian College Students with Pornography: How It Disrupts the Educational Process of Spiritual Formation" (PhD. diss., Biola University, 2005), 11.

60. William Beaver and Stephen Paul, "Internet Pornography: Variables Related to use Among Traditional-Aged College Students," *Sociological Viewpoints* (Fall 2011): 25.

61. Ibid., 8.

62. Amanda Frick, "The Acceptance and Usage of Pornography and its Effects on College Students' Risky Behaviors and Family Formation Values," University of New Hampshire Methods of Social Research (May 13, 2009): 19.

63. Steve Shadrach, *The Fuel and the Flame: 10 Keys to Ignite Your College Campus for Jesus Christ* (Waynesborough: Authentic Media, 2003), 39.

64. Webroot. "Internet Pornography by the Numbers; A Significant Threat to Society." Webroot. `http://www.webroot.com/En_US/consumer/tips/internet-pornography-by-the-numbers` (accessed July 7, 2013).

65. Leonard Sweet, *What Matters Most: How We Got the Point but Missed the Person*. Colorado Springs, CO: Waterbrook Press, 86-87.

66. This confidential information is asked in an application, which is then followed with several phone calls if necessary. For an example of a STINT application see `http://cruoncampus.org/go/international/why-consider-a-year-overseas/`

67. J. Herbert Kane, *Understanding Christian Mission* (Grand Rapids, MI: Baker Books House, 1978), 67.

68. Ahrend, 198.

69. Ibid.

70. Ahrend, 33.

71. John R. Mott, *The Pastor and Modern Missions: A Plea for Leadership in World Evangelization* (New York: Student Volunteer Movement, 1923), 172.

72. Todd Ahrend, *In This Generation*, 210.

73. Larry Osborne, *10 Dumb Things Smart Christians Believe* (Colorado Springs: Multnomah Books, 2009), 56.

74. Ibid.

75. DeYoung, *Just Do Something*, 63.

76. M. Blaine Smith, *Knowing God's Will: Finding Guidance for Personal Decisions* (Downers Grove: InterVarsity Press, 1991), 179.

77. Kane, *Understanding Christian Missions*, 39.

78. Robert E. Speer, "A Missionary Call," Traveling Team, `http://www.thetravelingteam.org/articles/missionary-call` (accessed April 4, 2013).

79. Ruth A. Tucker. *From Jerusalem to Irian Jaya: A Biographical History of Christian Missions* (Grand Rapids, MI: Zondervan), 2004.

Change

TOP International interns enjoy an elephant ride at their mid-year retreat in Thailand
LEFT Students praying for the campuses in Western Africa

OPPOSITE International intern helping serve a "Love Meal" to Syrian & North African refugees in Athens, Greece

Ένας αγώνας
για όλους
WIND

ABOVE Students bond over challenging times in India

TOP Worship celebration in Cote D'Ivoire
BELOW South Africa Summer Mission students enjoy a safari

OPPOSITE Students help build a women's dormitory on Summer Mission in Cape Town, South Africa

NORTHERN
COLORADO

OPPOSITE TOP Building friendships in South Asia
OPPOSITE BOTTOM International Intern discipling his new Ivorian brother in Christ

ABOVE TOP LEFT Intern with his new friend in South Africa
ABOVE TOP RIGHT Student and camper at an English camp in Slovakia
ABOVE BOTTOM Summer Mission students experience a church service in Western Africa

ABOVE Intern with his new Ivorian friend in Cote D'Ivoire

TOP Greek student reads scripture at a meeting in Athens
BOTTOM Students explore the streets of South Asia

TOP International Interns on the Polytechnic University campus in Greece

OPPOSITE TOP Staff member chatting with student in Bratislava, Slovakia
OPPOSITE BOTTOM Student uses an evangelistic tool, Soularium, to engage with Slovak high schoolers

LEFT Summer Mission students share a tearful goodbye in South Asia

ABOVE TOP Worship service held in Serbia

International intern with her sisters in Christ in the Ivory Coast